C000091541

Submissions Visit the *TSQ* home page (lgbt.arizona.edu/transgender-studies -quarterly) to see calls for papers for upcoming issues. Essays should be submitted for review to the journal's Editorial Manager page (editorialmanager.com/tsq/). We do not accept submissions of previously published work. Neither do we accept submissions that are under review or have been accepted for publication elsewhere. The journal uses the author-date form of citation as described in chapter 15 of *The Chicago Manual of Style*. To facilitate the anonymous review process, please include your name, affiliation, contact information, and any other identifying information on a separate cover page, and be sure that citations to your own work are worded to maintain your anonymity. We also welcome proposals for special issues on a particular theme. Visit the homepage of the *TSQ* editorial office for information about submitting a proposal for a special issue.

Reviews Contact the appropriate review or subject editor if you have a proposal or inquiry regarding a potential review subject. Please do not submit unsolicited reviews.

Arts & Culture Editor
Cáel Keegan, keeganc@gvsu.edu

Translation Editor
Cole Rizki, cr3np@virginia.edu

Book Review Editors
Chris Barcelos, chris.barcelos@umb.edu
LaVelle Ridley, laridley@umich.edu

Books for review may be sent to
Chris Barcelos
Department of Women's, Gender, and Sexualities
  Studies
University of Massachusetts Boston
Wheatley Hall, 100 Morrissey Blvd.
Boston, MA 02125

Subscriptions Direct all orders to Duke University Press, Journals Customer Relations, 905 W. Main St., Suite 18B, Durham, NC 27701. Annual subscription rates: print-plus-electronic institutions, $292; print-only institutions, $278; e-only institutions, $244; individuals, $45; students, $28. For information on subscriptions to the e-Duke Journals Scholarly Collections, contact libraryrelations@dukepress.edu. Print subscriptions: add $14 postage and applicable HST (including 5% GST) for Canada; add $18 postage outside the US and Canada. Back volumes (institutions): $278. Single issues: institutions, $70; individuals, $12. For more information, contact Duke University Press Journals at 888-651-0122 (toll-free in the US and Canada) or 919-688-5134; subscriptions@ dukeupress.edu.

Permissions Photocopies for course or research use that are supplied to the end user at no cost may be made without explicit permission or fee. Photocopies that are provided to the end user for a fee may not be made without payment of permission fees to Duke University Press. Send requests for permission to republish copyrighted material to permissions@dukeupress.edu.

Indexing For a list of the sources in which *TSQ* is indexed and abstracted, see dukeupress.edu /TSQ-Transgender-Studies-Quarterly.

Advertising Direct inquiries about advertising to Journals Advertising Coordinator, journals_ advertising@dukeupress.edu.

TSQ: Transgender Studies Quarterly (ISSN 2328-9252) is published four times a year by Duke University Press, 905 W. Main St., Suite 18B, Durham, NC 27701.

T*SQ Transgender Studies Quarterly

Volume 9 ★ Number 1 ★ February 2022

The t4t Issue

Edited by Cameron Awkward-Rich and Hil Malatino

BOOK REVIEWS

ABOUT THE COVER ART

Meanwhile, t4t

CAMERON AWKWARD-RICH and HIL MALATINO

I feel like I'm the only one with this problem—a gay man in a woman's body—
and so alone, so left out. I gather Jack Garland's remnants with delight + think of
his life compared to mine + it does make me feel better. But not much.
—Lou Sullivan, *We Both Laughed in Pleasure*

"What are you going to say to Ed?"
"I don't know. I want to know if she's OK. I just think we all shouldn't be fighting
each other. We need to stick together."
—Jess, in Leslie Feinberg's *Stone Butch Blues*

[Josh] got this look on his face with his eyes all big and blue and sad and understanding and loving all at once. He held out his arms and drew me in. "It's okay,
baby," he said, "it's okay. I'll take care of it. Don't worry about a thing. And he
didn't sound mad, not even a little bit.
        And that's when I knew it was time to run away again.
—The narrator in Kai Cheng Thom's *Fierce Femmes and Notorious Liars*

T4T is an ideal, I guess, and we fall short of it most of the time. But that's better
than before. All it took was the end of the world to make that happen.
—Zoey, in *Torrey Peter's Infect Your Friends and Loved Ones*

A necdotally, many of us are (and have been) t4t. But if you derive your sense of
trans worlds from academic writing and/or popular culture, this would be
easy enough to not know, fixated as these genres tend to be on the dramas of trans
people negotiating cis worlds of sense. When we proposed this special issue in late
October of 2019, it was clear to us that t4t as a concept and practice organizes some
of the most salient features of trans life and cultural/knowledge production but

TSQ: Transgender Studies Quarterly ∗ Volume 9, Number 1 ∗ February 2022   **1**
DOI 10.1215/23289252-9475467   © 2022 Duke University Press

that, at the same, it is largely underthought and untheorized within the interdisciplinary spaces of trans studies. Indeed, as Cassius Adair and Aren Aizura point out in their contribution to this special issue, the academic literature on trans sexualities has tended to assume the inevitability of trans-cis partnerings, even as anyone with a basic familiarity with past and present trans scenes knows that this assumption cannot hold. Many of the insights of this issue, then, might be obvious to anyone who lives a trans life. However, given the frequency with which submissions to this issue relied on one paragraph of one of our essays, an essay that is only marginally about t4t, one of the most important things this issue might do is offer a more varied set of citations for writing about what "some kind of we" already knows (Banias 2016: 3–4).

And yet, precisely because of the apparent transparency of t4t to anyone "in the know," we approached this editorial task deliberately holding the content of "t4t" as an open question and, perhaps more to the point, as a problem. As a bit of trans vernacular, *t4t* circulates within various contemporary trans intimate publics as if it were a neutral description of, for example, sexual practice or subcultural ethos. *T4t* circulates, that is, as if it merely described and did not also construct the (trans) world. To approach *t4t* as, instead, a question and a problem means asking what it is and does and might do. Has the circulation of something called t4t further reified cis/trans binaries and/or certain visions of "trans community," and to what effect? Is it useful to think about t4t as structuring practices of academic knowledge making and field habitus, something that might be implicit in the structure of *TSQ* and explicit in Cáel Keegan's (2020: 387–88) claim that "trans* studies can only thrive . . . in a situation that gives it space to break from the epistemic structure of women's studies and queer studies"? What is the relationship between t4t as an interpersonal form and t4t as an exploitable and marketable ethos that might be used to capitalize on trans isolation through the promise of community, euphoria, and bliss? How is the insider knowledge gleaned through t4t relationality being commodified in current iterations of trans-tech (Geffen and Howard 2021)? How has the deployment (and, often, the idealization) of t4t distracted from or covered over the significant axes of difference, race chief among them, that characterize and trouble trans affinities and solidarities?

T4t means, most basically, trans-for-trans. The term arose in the context of early 2000s Craigslist personals, working to both sequester trans folks from the categories of "m" and "w" and enable some kind of us to find one another for hookups. However, while the term is linked to Craigslist, the overlapping things that it presently names—trans separatist social forms, trans × trans erotics, trans practices of mutual aid and emotional support—have been most robustly theorized within trans literature and other forms of cultural production that both predate and outlast the Craigslist personal, from the mimeographed trans news-letters and zines of the latter half of the twentieth century to the work of con-temporary trans authors like Casey Plett, Kai Cheng Thom, and Torrey Peters. And what is obvious from such writing—as well as the term's origin—is that t4t resists idealization. T4t sex, desire, erotics, and social practices are nothing if not fraught, animated by tension and contradiction, riven by complex forms of triggering and retraumatization. Practices of t4t love, desire, connection, and support are simultaneously imperative and deeply difficult to cultivate and maintain.

For this reason, each of our framing epigraphs is drawn from a literary scene of what might be considered failed t4t, insofar as these are scenes in which trans sociality cannot ameliorate the affective and/or material deprivation that saturates trans life under racial capitalism and trans antagonism. In the first, Lou Sullivan (writing in the late 1980s) expresses a common impulse animating work in trans history: an attempt to ameliorate the sense of aloneness and onliness that attends many trans lives in the absence of ready-to-hand history and community. But while it remains a commonplace of trans history to narrate itself as a project of caring for the trans present, Sullivan is, like Heather Love, unsure about the possibility of "emotional rescue" (Love 2007: 31). Researching Jack Garland and telling a story about Garland as a proto-gay-trans-man makes Sullivan (2019: 332) "feel better"—that is, less alone in the world—"but not much." This "but not much" should alert us to the fact that t4t as a self-making and self-sustaining research practice both undergirds the foundations of what is now trans studies and fails to ameliorate the real affective needs that drive so many of us to such projects in the first place. Such reparatively driven projects of historical recovery offer lukewarm comfort, at best; you can't cuddle, fuck, or trauma-bond with specters. Nevertheless, t4t socialities seem to always be composed, in part, out of intangible and virtual resources. On t4t as a form of virtual sociality and kin-ship, Amira Lundy-Harris's contribution to this issue explores how encounters with trans textual artifacts (specifically, trans memoirs) help produce and actualize trans selves. Lundy-Harris articulates how trans folks are so often assisted in self-making by texts authored by people, both still and no longer living, that "we may never meet but who still help move us toward the trans self we know ourselves to be." He points us to the importance of a practice of reading across trans dif-ferences in search of resonance, and he positions this practice as integral to trans becoming. We might even call it a t4t reading practice.

But Lundy-Harris also points us to the racial logic of many deployments of t4t. Namely, when taken as an uncritical utopian horizon or an a priori ethi-cal form, t4t can cover over—and so reinforce—white racial dominance. In our second epigraph from *Stone Butch Blues*, for example, Leslie Feinberg's protag-onist Jess is responding to the news of a barfight that was sparked by Grant's (a white butch) racist commentary on the Vietnam War and Martin Luther King Jr.'s assassination and Edwin's—the lone Black butch in the novel—refusal to put up with it. The incident, in turn, resulted in the temporary barring of Black people from the bar, from the novel's primary scene of social life. On hearing about the fight, Jess immediately deploys the ideal of t4t as a way of smoothing over differences between butches in order to preserve their *we*; she wants to remind Edwin, not Grant, that "we need to stick together" (Feinberg 2003: 126). Although, in this scene, Jess's longing for an uncomplicated *we* is portrayed as naive, it's also true that Jess's narrative trajectory comes at Edwin's expense, insofar as Edwin functions throughout as a learning opportunity, a doomed device of Jess's characterization, even as the novel glimpses the trans of Black trans studies that Lundy-Harris describes. In short, Jess and Edwin's t4t friendship prefigures the generative and vexed dynamic highlighted in the introduction to "The Issue of Blackness" of *TSQ*, wherein "the field of transgender studies, like other fields, seems to use this Black subject as a springboard to move toward other things, presumably white things" (Ellison et al. 2017: 162).

Our third epigraph captures a similar dynamic within t4t, narrated from the trans woman of color's perspective. In this scene, the unnamed narrator of Kai Cheng Thom's *Fierce Femmes and Notorious Liars* recounts the moment that sparks her final flight within and from the novel's frame. This time, rather than fleeing from her parents' house to transition and live among other trans women, the narrator is fleeing from her short-lived romance with Josh, a monied, white, kind, university-bred trans man. Importantly, the narrator's relationship with Josh was a nourishing one; it provided a holding space in which she could test out a vision of her future and experience sexual pleasure relatively unguarded by her defenses against past and potential trauma, violation, and dysphoria. At the same time, it's clear from the quoted scene, in which the narrator has just broken Josh's television, that Josh does not exactly relate to the narrator as a person but, rather, as an ideal, something that can do no wrong. Josh's uncritical, accepting response to her actions seems predicated on an objectifying, depersonalized lionization of trans women of color that serves as a caricature that confirms his white saviorship. His lack of anger is grounded in an interpretation of her as fundamentally trau-matized and perennially prone to lashing out; the situational specificity of her affective response, and his role in it, are sidelined by his overdetermined scripting of their relationship, one in which they are an interracial "trans power couple" and he is the white providential figure who saves her from herself and secures, with his intergenerational wealth, educational privilege, and benevolent support, both her financial and emotional security. No wonder she recoils. It is, again, precisely the apparent absence of conflict that marks this scene of t4t as both a site of seductive ease and of profound trouble.

Rather than think of all of the above as depictions of failed t4t or failures to be "properly" t4t, we might instead follow the wisdom of Peters's (2016: 67, 55) *Infect Your Friends and Loved Ones* which insists that t4t "for real"—in an ideal or even "better" iteration—would require the end of the world but might, as a concept for the meanwhile, provide (for some of us, sometimes) places of rest, generative conflict, a bit of pleasure, scenes to run away from with a better sense of why we are running. This nonideal, nonutopic sense of t4t is honed in and through the multivalent crises of the present. The more intensively a tenuous trans *we* is structurally disenfranchised, maligned, and abandoned, the more necessary t4t praxis becomes; the more structurally disenfranchised, maligned, and abandoned this *we* is, the more angst, trauma, mistrust, and fear of abandonment we bring to t4t relationalities. But this coincides with reprieve, mutual (if always partial) knownness, and pleasure. Even the internecine friction and baggage deepens, at least potentially, collective knowledge of the risks and limits of and barriers to intimate connection, solidarity, and coalition.

Ultimately, many of the essays in this special issue regard t4t this way, as a provisional, tense, sometimes violent, and always fraught form in the meanwhile. Nicholas Tyler Reich's loving study of Tiffany Saint-Bunny's photo project *Truck Sluts*, for example, turns on t4t (and t4t*) as "trouble" and techniques for staying with it. Reich reads Saint-Bunny's aesthetic practice as multiply t4t—simultaneously "a desirous exchange . . . between trans media makers and trans audiences," between trans people and trucks, and "between trans bodies, oil, and petro-machinery." By situating *Truck Sluts* within a larger conversation about the interrelations of gender, fossil fuel, and climate crisis, they offer it as an archive that, through disidentifying with the "white-nationalist petro-masculinit[ies]" that undergird the dystopias of the present, makes thinkable queer/trans "trashy environmentalisms" that take sometimes toxic enmeshment and apparently compromising pleasures seriously. The toxic and dystopian aspects of t4t itself are, in turn, explicated in Amy Marvin's contribution, which focuses on the rise and fall of Topside Press as a scene of trans cultural production explicitly organized by the ethos of t4t. Marvin hones in on the way that such idealized and institutionalized deployments of t4t often actively enable and cover over abuse, exclusion, and exploitation while claiming to contest these very things. Given this, she wisely insists that t4t "require[s] some hesitation and caution against overreach" because it cannot be understood as "fully separable from the many ways that care can become short-circuited between trans and cis people." Chris Barcelos likewise regards trans crowdfunding, a common form of potentially t4t support, as compromised or "complicit care." Expanding on their earlier work on trans GoFundMe campaigns, Barcelos reminds us that these campaigns distribute material and emotional support unevenly, in ways that both mirror and reproduce existing inequality and structures of domination. For this reason, "t4t crowdfunding is more successful as an affective care practice than a wealth redistribution effort"; like Marvin, Barcelos invites cautious and careful thinking "about what it can and cannot do for our collective liberation."

In light of all of the above, here are our t4t failures: this issue is composed exclusively of writers working in the United States, is notably trans masc-heavy in authorship and trans femme in object, and contains several contributors who are our collaborators and friends. Some of this is about decisions we made, decisions to prioritize more standard academic writing in the print issue and curate a supplemental open genre folio on *TSQ*Now*, to see what came in rather than solicit. Some of it is about our particular networks and disciplinary positioning. Some of it is about the structure of *TSQ* and the academy writ large. Much of it is about the sheer absurdity of attempting to conduct business as usual during the COVID-19 pandemic, uprisings in the summer of 2020, attempted coup of January 2021, legislative attacks on trans youth and reproductive rights, and other ongoing, everyday crises of late capitalism. That is, it is reflective of the inherent failures of t4t in the interregnum, before the end of the world, in the midst of a resolutely nonideal present (Malatino 2019). We might say, then, that this issue theorizes, exemplifies, and reproduces the problem of t4t as it manages to signal something like a critical trans politics while often actually failing to create and/or sustain relationally across other vectors of difference, exacerbating forms of segregation and extraction, and being shot through with intramural hostilities and abuse. But t4t is also necessary for the elaboration of trans subjectivities and lifeworlds.

The integral role t4t sex plays in these processes is astutely (and sometimes hilariously) theorized by Adair and Aizura, who read transmasc4transmasc porn to theorize trans sex as a crucial site of trans becoming. Critically countering contemporary transphobic accounts of rapid onset gender dysphoria as a form of trans contagion, they ask, in effect, what's so bad about trans contagion? They write that in the current climate of trans panic (especially around trans youth), "it may feel difficult to admit that in fact, yes, many of us discovered we were trans through being seduced by a trans person. . . . Or, at the very least, by finding a trans person unbearably hot." But t4t sex between trans mascs (and trans femmes) has nevertheless long held the status of something like an open secret among us: underdiscussed or elided in public-facing conversations about trans sexuality but (surreptitiously or unabashedly) practiced by many. Adair and Aizura insist on the centrality of sex in any understanding of t4t, building an archive of late twentieth- and twenty-first-century ftm4ftm erotica and porn and investigating how the Daddy/boy and group sex dynamics depicted within this archive operate "as gender labor, affective and intersubjective work that produces gender and that in t4t erotics works within a framework of differentiated reciprocity."

Similarly highlighting the imperative work of t4t in shaping and supporting trans arts of living, V. Jo Hsu reads *TransGriot*, the online archive of
the late Monica Roberts, as a "blueprint for t4t love-politics," which Hsu theorizes
as "transformational care based in openness toward and responsibility for one
another." Stressing Roberts's commitment to an ethos of witnessing and mutual
vulnerability, Hsu reads her archive as a vivid example of t4t care that refuses to
shy away from difficult conversations across the journalistic, Black, and trans
communities in which Roberts situated herself. She consistently stressed mutual
accountability and the importance of calling folks in, from cis gay and lesbian
journalists who misgender and deadname, to Black social justice organizations
that fail to prioritize the needs of Black trans subjects, to white trans folks per-
petuating racism within trans communal and movement spaces. Hsu describes
this ethos as one that "prioritizes trans kinship and lives while also honoring
trans people's embeddedness in other social and political communities," one that
mobilizes "t4t care toward a more just world while embracing the fact that care
itself is a fraught, imperfect, and ongoing process."

Fraught, imperfect, and ongoing: this is perhaps the best characterization
of t4t praxis in this long meanwhile that a "tarnished, / problematic, and certainly
uneven" trans *we* inhabit, living as we do sometime after some supposed tipping
point but a long way off from anything resembling justice (Banias 2016: 4). T4t
can offer so much: some measure of respite, a break from cis-centric optics and
assumptions, a relation through which we might learn more about what we want
to become, what we desire, how we want to live in these so often fraught body-
minds, mutually actualizing touch, a little room to breathe just a bit easier, perhaps.
But, as so many of the essays here remind us, it is also a crucible through which
we come to learn just how opaque we remain to one another, just how intensively
we've internalized the lessons taught by trans antagonism, just how difficult it is to
see, love, want, fuck, support, and simply be with one another. Whether these
tough recognitions are failures or lessons, though, depends on what we (fraught,
imperfect, ongoing) do next.

References

Banias, Ari. 2016. *Anybody*. New York: W. W. Norton.
Ellison, Treva, Kai M. Green, Matt Richardson, and C. Riley Snorton. 2017. "We Got Issues:
    Toward a Black Trans*/Studies." *TSQ* 4, no. 2: 162–69.
Feinberg, Leslie. 2003. *Stone Butch Blues*. Los Angeles: Alyson.
Geffen, Sasha, and Annie Howard. 2021. "Quantifying Transition." *Baffler*, March 22. thebaffler
    .com/latest/quantifying-transition-geffen-howard.
Keegan, Cáel M. 2020. "Getting Disciplined: What's Trans* about Queer Studies Now?" *Journal of
    Homosexuality* 67, no. 3: 384–97.

Love, Heather. 2007. *Feeling Backward: Loss and the Politics of Queer History*. Cambridge, MA: Harvard University Press.

Malatino, Hil. 2019. "Future Fatigue: Trans Intimacies and Trans Presents (or How to Survive the Interregnum)." *TSQ* 6, no. 4: 635–58.

Peters, Torrey. 2016. *Infect Your Friends and Loved Ones*. Self-published.

Sullivan, Louis. 2019. *We Both Laughed in Pleasure: The Selected Diaries of Lou Sullivan, 1961–1991*. Edited by Ellis Martin and Zach Ozma. New York: Nightboat.

Thom, Kai Cheng. 2018. *Fierce Femmes and Notorious Liars: A Dangerous Trans Girl's Confabulous Memoir*. Montreal: Metonymy.

Short-Circuited Trans Care, t4t, and Trans Scenes

AMY MARVIN

Abstract This essay discusses short-circuited trans care by focusing on failures of t4t as an ethos both interpersonally and within particular trans scenes. The author begins by recounting an experience working at a bar/restaurant that appealed to its identity as a caring trans community space as part of its exploitation of trans workers. This dynamic inspires the main argument, that t4t can become an ethos of scenes and institutions beyond the interpersonal while short-circuiting practices of trans care. Short-circuited trans care is then traced to t4t by drawing from Hil Malatino's work on trans care and t4t, Kai Cheng Thom's work on community dynamics, and trans literature to argue that practices of t4t often include abuse, expulsion, and assumptive care. This short-circuited trans care is linked to trans scenes by discussing the ethos of t4t in the history of Topside Press and trans cultural production. The author does not condemn t4t and to this effect offers a critique of tethering trans cultural production to prestige instead of care. Rather, the goal of this essay is to openly discuss aspects of t4t and trans care that are often obscured through the projection of a highly questionable "we" or universalized "trans community."

Keywords trans theory, trans literature, trans care, care ethics, feminist philosophy

> Fuck t4t.
> —Torrey Peters, *Infect Your Friends and Loved Ones*

Trans Theory as Disgruntled Employee Theory

In late 2018 after I finished my dissertation defense, my advisor asked why I looked so drained rather than excited. Stripped of its glamour, my PhD was not a reward but a sign that I would no longer be eligible for academic employment at the university where I had taught for seven years. I was thus reset to the condition that drove me to accept going to graduate school in the first place: a productive college career that inevitably leads to a search for extreme underemployment to avoid unemployment.

TSQ: Transgender Studies Quarterly ★ Volume 9, Number 1 ★ February 2022 **9**
DOI 10.1215/23289252-9475481 © 2022 Duke University Press

Still living in a sprawling college pseudo-city and not yet able to move, I had few options for a job that would make the rent. Most trans women in the city worked at a call center that paid $10–$12 an hour part-time, but it was on a day-labor system that included frequent layoffs. Through a mutual friend, my girlfriend and I were able to get jobs at a local gay bar—sorry, LGBTQIA+ venue—that had recently opened downtown.

Initially being a part of the space of the upstart "not just a gay bar" felt like being part of something special for the community, especially as it was focused on trans community. The owner was nonbinary, the bathrooms were gender neutral, there were several trans employees who had difficulty getting hired elsewhere in the supposedly welcoming city, there were portraits of trans women on some of the walls, the bookshelf had several books of trans writing, and sometimes Anohni could be heard from the closet-sized kitchen. It was envisioned as just the beginning of a larger and much-needed nonprofit queer- and trans-focused community center with everything employee owned. The space was thus advertised as uniquely for trans people and by trans people while serving the broader community. We did not take the restaurant job to be utopian, since the nature of bar/restaurant/event work caused tensions and was frequently demanding, but we nonetheless held onto a unique trans-for-trans vision that we thought could improve our community.

The reality of the space despite its good intentions ended up even worse than working at a typical low-wage bar, restaurant, or event-planning job, including the interpersonal difficulties that often arise from such work. The rhetoric of creating an inclusive space turned into the usual capitalist idealization of the "self-made" small business without workers, with low wages, irregular or cut hours, and pressure to serve food or ingredients that were past date to patrons. The rhetoric of community also fed into the pressure to sacrifice for the space, to not speak up about sexual harassment, and to expel workers who did not fall in line or could not keep up. What I thought had been a trans-for-trans space was instead a nightmare under the capitalist conditions through which it emerged. At the same time, my partner and I were getting ghosted by the local clinic that was advertised as an exceptional trans-friendly space because they refused to prescribe trans women adequate levels of estrogen, suggesting that it made trans women crazy.

It occurred to me while working in this supposedly for-us space, while nursing burns, standing out in the cold because my shift was wrongly scheduled, getting kissed by a superior on the face, refusing to serve old leftovers or spoiled cream cheese to patrons, watching my girlfriend get paid under the table to not speak up about sexual harassment, and having trans coworkers disappear to be told later they had been stealing or violent, that perhaps this was part of the fabric of t4t spaces rather than an aberration. When idealized and institutionalized, the otherwise quirky and negative elements of t4t became exacting and cruel. I began to grow weary of appeals such as "we're a family," "we're a community," "this is for us," and "why are you trying to damage this space?"

While working in the kitchen, my thoughts often turned to the intellectual traditions of the institutions I was now locked out of while serving their graduate student and professor clientele. In their essay "Contingent Foundations" Judith Butler (1995) defends the compatibility between democratic feminist politics and deconstructive critique by focusing on the continuous fragmentation within feminism that results from calling for a coherent feminist collective. Butler specifically focuses on the reference to a "we" within feminist politics, a feminist "we" that rhetorically seeks a feminist "unity" and "integrity," uniting the subject of women for a collective struggle and collective liberation (48). Butler points out that this feminist "we" and the "common element" of the feminist subject has rightfully been challenged as racist, as colonialist, as essentializing, and as exclusionary (48–50), giving rise to a perpetual anxiety over the efficacy of feminism without a centralizing normative authority, as well as the continued challenge of deconstructive critique to the subject of feminism. Challenging a coherent referent subject and "we" of feminism is not a call to scrap collectivity; instead, it acknowledges collectivity as a site of difference and contestation in which even the most well-meaning projection of an inclusive "we" can be constituted through exclusions and papered-over omissions.

There is something funny about starting off a trans theory essay in the 2020s with a citation of Judith Butler after trans theory has so long been tethered to discussions of queer theory and the work of Butler specifically, a citational move that could be cast as both naive and stale (cf. Namaste 2019). In part, I turn to Butler for a second sailing of critique, a hopeful revisiting of new affinities in light of concretized cynicism, and a gesture of openness prefacing a conversation that may be interpreted as at best divisive and at worst mean. Mainly, I turn to Butler as a reminder of the long-standing limitations of politics in the service of a projected cohesive body or community, which is all too easy to shed or soften through the hopefulness and positive sentiments of t4t and its related projects of cultural production.

Coincidentally, my personal reflection on t4t spaces and the communal "we" has already risked commitment to a category error. Was I even correct in thinking of the restaurant space as a t4t space, or is t4t necessarily interpersonal and not institutional? Furthermore, by receiving such cruel treatment in this t4t space, did it no longer constitute a t4t space, or had it never truly realized itself as t4t? In this essay I seek to clarify these ironies of t4t as an ethos. First, I link t4t with harm, abuse, and expulsion by referencing Hil Malatino's work on trans care and t4t, then I link it with Kai Cheng Thom's work on abuse and community. I point out the risks of covering over abuse and taking part in short-circuited assumptive care as part of the ethos of t4t rather than an aberration. Then, through a brief and careful discussion of the history of Topside Press, I argue that t4t can manifest in t4t spaces and institutions that are likewise susceptible to short-circuited care, abuse, and expulsion. I do not intend to present a final word against t4t but instead suggest that t4t can go horribly wrong, and I want to emphasize that people who experience t4t going horribly wrong are not hostile and deluded. Trans people frequently, deeply hurt other trans people both interpersonally and through institutions in ways that challenge reconciliation and community.

Interpersonal t4t, Abuse, and Assumptive Care

In his book *Trans Care*, Malatino (2020) places an emphasis on care among trans people as a necessary but fraught practice. Drawing from trans elder Rupert Raj's discussion of "voluntary" gender work and its connection with burnout, Malatino points out that trans care is usually unpaid, unsupported, difficult, and exhausting (21–23). Furthermore, Malatino emphasizes that practices of trans care go beyond the individualized and discrete scope constraining the concept of burnout, taking place instead within mutual communities that share negative affect and trauma even as they share the care necessary to sustain each other (23, 25). Understanding trans care thus requires a more diffuse, mutual, communal, and tempered framework of care as a practice, analyzing not only the worlds enabled through care but also the tensions and fragmentations caused by a profound lack of support.

Malatino's (2019) analysis of trans care as an unsupported and fraught practice carries over to his earlier essay on t4t, "Future Fatigue." Meditating on the complicated and affectively challenging temporalities of transition, Malatino turns to t4t specifically as a sustaining practice of love and care in the fraught "interregnum" of trans life (647). He discusses Thom's book *Fierce Femmes and Notorious Liars* and Torrey Peters's novella *Infect Your Friends and Loved Ones* as examples of "speculative dystopia" that challenge the present while also refusing to project a pleasant, uncomplicated dream of the future (647–48). Malatino argues that the narrative of Thom's book, presented as a memoir while also thwarting the idealized narrative expected of trans memoirs, focuses on "trans femmes living and loving alongside one another," including mutual support, mutual conflict, and resistance (649–51).

Malatino also draws from Peters's work as an uptake of "t4t," as it was taken beyond its use for Craiglist personals to the more "politicized and erotic" yet contingent separatism it has been associated with in recent years. Malatino writes,

> t4t emerges from a recognition that trans subjects, too, might benefit from a sev-
> ering of ties to cissexist modes of interpellating trans bodies (as failures, fakes,

inorganic, inauthentic), and, moreover, that such strategic separatism might be one of the most direct routes toward cultivating self-love, self-regard, and self-care, especially because it confronts and disrupts the assimilationist logics that structure the limiting forms of individuated futural aspiration already discussed. The hope is that, in community with one another, insulated—however temporarily—from cissexist modes of perception, some significant healing might be possible. (654)

Malatino locates in t4t a frequently erotic and politicized dynamic of care among trans people, cobbled together in an uncertain present and galvanized toward an equally uncertain future. In addition to the contingent care and political spaces it offers, Malatino argues that Peters's vision of t4t is "cynical, skeptical, . . . set up to fail" while embracing "ethical imperfection and complexity" (656). Furthermore, t4t may involve interpersonal difficulties among trans people, including "envy, annoyance, jealousy, and judgment," shaped in the intersection between survival and scarcity. By referencing Thom's and Peters's work, Malatino strives to go beyond flattened pictures of "the trans community" that ignore differences among trans people, focusing on key practices of care and love while also refusing to gloss over tensions, aggressions, and bad feelings (656–57).

One of the strengths of Malatino's work, in addition to the breadth he considers and his philosophical attentiveness to contemporary trans conversations, is that he acknowledges the great difficulties of sustaining trans care and the many fractures that accompany a practice of t4t. In this essay, I want to focus specifically on the negative, ruptured side of t4t both interpersonally and in the realm of cultural production. While I agree with Malatino that trans care is necessary, difficult, and often fractured, I have found through experience that dynamics of t4t can also perpetuate abuse or false projections of community that go beyond his analysis. I want to sit with the ways that t4t as an ethos gets stretched to the point of shattering, when the care it offers short-circuits or is twisted to harm, and when its ideal gets defended over the actual people it may have connected. First, I focus specifically on abuse through Thom's work, and then I draw out elements of trans literature that express more of an ambivalence for projects of t4t and trans care than Malatino addresses.

Thom critically analyzes queer and trans community and the propensity for abuse, including abuse coverups in her book *I Hope We Choose Love*. Thom (2019: 53) opens her discussion of intracommunity violence with a description of queer community as a sacred space called Queerlandia:

> In this fabulous, fictional Queerlandia, we are free—free from the oppression of the often violent and neglectful families and communities where we were raised.

In Queerlandia, we imagine, no one is exploited or beaten or raped. No one is excluded. No one is ignored. In Queerlandia, our politics are woke and our words are revolutionary. We are free to love ourselves, to love others—to be loved, most crucial of all.

Like Malatino, Thom points out that the reality of queer and trans spaces is instead a messy and complicated one, full of people who are not prepared to discuss "the reality of bad things happening among us," including how to talk openly and heal (53). Abuse among LGBT people is thus often understood as a matter of casting out individuals or simply not saying anything (53–55).

Despite frequent discussions of safety, accountability, and dynamics of abuse, Thom argues that abuse remains a part of the obscured fabric of real Queerlandia, with the removal of called-out abusers often resulting in an expulsion that does not prevent other ongoing abusive dynamics (57–59). Frequently, expulsions from queer and trans community happen along the axis of race, class, and gender, with more severe callouts having little impact and less severe callouts resulting in others getting banished from queer spaces according to relative intracommunity marginalization (74). Even when Queerlandia is not taken as a utopia, its internal negativity requires dialogue and action beyond incorporating the inevitability of bad feelings in its ethos.

If grounded Queerlandia has issues of intracommunity harm, abuse, and expulsion, then interpersonal t4t is at risk for these dynamics as well. *Infect* acknowledges this when the protagonist is stabbed by her ex against her will, is called an "abuser" by her ex behind her back as a means of ostracization, and has a date with a trans man who raises the specter of the oversensitive trans woman to rile her up so she can get dismissed (Peters 2016a: 19, 39, 41). After all, the cover of *Infect* features a dead pig carcass with "t4t" carved into its head. Peters's earlier novella *The Masker* also depicts a fundamental break in bonds when a trans fem calls casino security guards to remove a trans woman at the behest of an abusive hookup, the titular masker of the story (Peters 2016b: 66–67). Peters is thus at times critical and ambivalent about t4t, explaining in an interview, "The book [*Infect*] . . . is about how hard that project [of t4t] can become, and what you gain and *what you lose* when you make a worldview that is entirely trans" (Peters: 2016c; emphasis mine).

In addition to t4t involving dynamics of abuse, silence, and expulsion, the identification with and for other trans people that it involves risks making incorrect assumptions that short-circuit practices of trans care. Imogen Binnie's 2013 novel *Nevada* depicts such an assumption when the main character Maria tries to convince James H to transition. James H ultimately concludes that the trans woman protagonist does not care about him beyond treating him like a project and decides to steal half of her heroin (Binnie 2013b: 236, 241–42). In an interview, Binnie (2013a) explained, "The sad thing at the center of the story of Maria and James, for me, is that Maria—by trying to hurry James along on starting to transition—sets him back. Probably years . . . Maria shows up, makes everything all about herself, and kind of tells James to shut up when he brings up the things he needs to work through." Even if this character transitioned later, the care practiced by Maria toward James H short-circuits their interaction through its arrogance, acting as an imposition and prescription rather than making a better attempt to listen to James H on his own terms.

Although nontrans people are frequently charged with paternalism against trans people, trans people are also at risk at making assumptions about the thoughts, feelings, and needs of other trans people, with an even deeper failure possible across power differences between differently situated trans people. Assumptive care among trans people may involve paternalism and an assertion of similarity that acknowledges difference but also goes too far in its imposition (see Marvin 2019). Taking up t4t as a larger ethos thus risks not only conflict but also moments when people project assumptions about care onto another, perhaps in the name of some overarching construct called "trans community" or "trans culture." A necessary component of discussing t4t is thus that trans people seriously hurt other trans people, sometimes despite or even because of good intentions.

t4t and Trans Cultural Production

Alongside the rise in popularity of t4t in the early to mid-2010s was a drive to create something called transgender literature, presented as an emerging and connected movement that harnessed the vision of trans people writing their work with and for other trans people rather than for mainstream nontrans audiences. In 2012 a new trans press called Topside published their debut book titled *The Collection: Short Fiction from the Transgender Vanguard* featuring twenty-eight short stories by twenty-eight trans authors. The introduction to the book, written by editors Tom Léger and Riley MacLeod (2012: 1), lamented their limited space and inability to include more trans authors, but they took the high volume of talented submissions as a promising sign for a revision to the field of trans literature after it had stagnated under nontrans control. The editors focused on the ability of the stories in the volume to center trans people in their stories, with each character a "principal actor," "agent of their own destiny," and "protagonist" with "real lives." Instead of serving as "comic relief," the trans character of *The Collection* develops throughout the story, an agent instead of an afterthought, with emotions, imagination, and a dynamic interaction with their world (2). The editors concluded with the hope that centering trans characters would "take trans art to its new iteration" and inspire possibilities for new trans authors while asking the reader "what's next?" for the future of trans literature (2–3).

In the very back of *The Collection*, past the author and editor biographies, Léger wrote an afterword titled "Know Thy Work," which presented a prophetic vision of the world of trans lit emerging on the horizon of Topside Press. Léger (2012: 89–90) describes the collective "act of labor" and resulting "body of literature" contained in *The Collection* as an unprecedented moment that has "never been seen or conceived of before," produced through "the will to work" and "the literal struggle to know" while offering "the beginnings of an investigation into a new world of thought." He contrasts this "new age" with stagnant "memoirs, political tracts, and . . . medical texts" that permit only objectifying, "positive," or "sympathetic" trans representation (90–92). Previous discourses failed to center trans people as realized subjects, in contrast to the new trans literature.

Topside Press's vision of a "new age" for trans lit was further developed in a 2013 zine advancing their focus from the centered trans agent-protagonist to a style of writing arising from interpersonal connections between trans writers and other trans people. Cowritten by Léger and MacLeod, *Is There a Transgender Text in This Class?* (2013: 2–7) broadly described trans lit as "products and artifacts of transgender culture" while advertising specifically to nontrans literature instructors. To contrast their publications with works focused on nontrans audiences, the authors shared a litmus test they call "The Topside Test," drawing from Alison Bechdel:

- Does the book include more than one trans character?
- Do they know each other?
- Do they talk to each other about something besides a transition-related medical procedure? (5)

The Topside Press zine argued that trans lit distinctly includes the presence of trans people who know each other and have discussions beyond transition, an indication that the author is familiar with trans people beyond the orbit of limited and distorting nontrans curiosity and that they are willing to write about this. The vision for the "new world" of trans lit was shaping up to center not only trans subjects but also connection, with trans people occupying a lifeworld that includes and centers other trans people.

In a 2014 essay Katherine Cross contrasted the "renaissance of trans women's literature" represented by Topside Press and Biyuti Publishing, which focused on writing by trans women of color, with the tradition of the trans memoir

written for nontrans audiences. Rather than present the mid-2010s trans literature moment as a radical break, Cross (2014) linked it with histories of writing
shared among trans people, arguing,

> For decades, we chatted on AIM, networked on LiveJournal, met in bars, and lent
> ever more of our fire to the long-running insurgent medium of zines. We learned
> to write from other women who wrote in lightning, iron, and blood. Many of us
> cut our teeth in role-playing games and multi-user dungeons, while still others had
> writing collectives . . . and too many others were alone but for the solace found on
> bookshelves and during late nights on the computer.

For Cross, trans literature was distinct because of the unprecedented opportunity
for trans women to have their existing writing finally elevated beyond the con-
sumption of a nontrans audience.

A year later Casey Plett (2015) published "Rise of the Gender Novel" to
critique the stagnant forms that trans people had been forced into in nontrans
literature, which included the isolation of trans characters from other trans
people. Plett wrote of cis-penned trans characters, "Each protagonist is a chosen
one, a lone wolf plodding on against adversity. They do no wrong; they remain
stoic and gentle in the face of difficulty." Plett (2015) argued that such characters
fail to reach the real lives of trans people, let alone consider trans people as
readers. In an early 2016 conversation, T Clutch Fleischmann and Torrey Peters
discussed the importance of a trans audience for literature that refuses cardboard
cutout trans characters, drawing from critiques by Topside Press. Peters explained
that rethinking the audience of trans literature as trans not only required going
deeper into the complexities of trans life but also discussing "dirty laundry" and
ethical conflicts that would have otherwise been sanitized or simply not considered (Peters and Fleischmann 2016). Connection between trans people was thus a
key theme for the current and emerging trans lit scene as a means of advancing
past flattened nontrans writing.

The elevation of ongoing trans writing, the repositioning of trans people
as the subject of stories, and the emphasis on writing about and for a populated
trans lifeworld also fostered conversations about inspiring and nurturing trans
writers. Discussing Topside Press in a 2014 interview, Ryka Aoki (2014: 14) mentioned that the trans lit scene and Topside Press specifically were beginning to
recognize the need to "nurture artists." The call for the inspiring "new age" would
require a practice of nurturance and hence care for the emerging community of
trans writers. Topside Press attempted to bring more writers under their wing in
2016 with the formation of the Trans Women's Writing Workshop, inviting twenty-
six trans women writers to workshop their writing at Brooklyn College with other

trans women writers in the style of Lambda Literary Writer's Retreats (cf. Valens 2016). The workshop was a key moment for Topside Press as it built its publishing scene. The press aimed to cultivate a new crop of trans writers and a new framework that would foster connections between these writers, ultimately fulfilling Topside Press's call for a new wave of for-trans, by-trans publications.

The primary ethos of cultural production developed by Topside Press fits Malatino's (2019: 653–54) description of t4t: a politicized, often eroticized, and contingent separatist space that offers care, love, and healing while resisting cis-sexist assimilation. Beyond an interpersonal framework, this ethos can be taken up in the mode of trans cultural production, offering a space where trans people make work for other trans people to raise consciousness and build institutions of production such as publishing houses or queer/trans venues beyond cissexist limitations. Rachel Anne Williams (2019: 238) explicitly brings t4t into this mode, writing, "T4t is about solidarity. I want to make space to support trans lives, businesses, start-ups, relationships, artists, communes, spaces, political organizations, politicians, movements, and so on. t4t is by trans, for trans." In Topside, t4t had expanded into the realm of publishing, but the cohesiveness of "by trans, for trans" was swiftly challenged for casting too wide a net before the press and its vision quietly receded.

The Eternal Irony of "Trans Community"

Before continuing this essay, I offer a key aside about the caring practice of the critic, as Cameron Awkward-Rich's (2020: 39–40) work directs us toward. In this critical essay I am not attempting to provide a complete and detailed account of trans literature writ large; rather, I wish to focus on a few specific moments. In what follows, I am choosing to leave out parts of the story either because they do not fit the focus of this essay or out of respect for privacy. Additionally, I do not want to tether all of the people discussed with the fate and faults of Topside Press, which has been effectively defunct for several years. Finally, I want to acknowledge that Topside does not own t4t or trans-for-trans community spaces and publishing. We might consider, for example, the film *Gender Troublemakers* by Mirha-Soleil Ross and Xanthra Phillippa (1993), which was released far before Topside. Even t4t among trans people at the time of Topside Press was not fully captured by it. Instead, I am referring to Topside as an intensive scene of t4t as an ethos that resulted in short-circuited care vis-à-vis cultural production, even as we may still continue to respect work that emerged from and against its orbit.

Even prior to the Trans Women's Writing Workshop in 2016, Peters's novella projects acknowledged that trans women's writing needed to be circulated beyond Topside Press. In summer 2016 before the workshop, Peters described her novella projects as part of a larger future for trans novellas and self-publishing that could go beyond reliance on a press. These novellas were thus also "an elevator pitch" for boosting different trans voices through the quicker pace of self-publishing (Peters 2016d; see also Peters 2021). While discussing the novella *Infect* with Thom in 2017, Peters (2017) continued to laud self-publishing, emphasizing, "You don't need a perfectly clean text, you don't need an editor, you don't need a press, all you really need is a will to write and an account with some self-publishing platform." Beyond Topside and often entirely without it, trans publishing thus often included a trans-for-trans ethos, with considerations of how to break through the homogenizing effect of Topside as a rising publisher for trans work.

Back in the 2016 interview, Peters wondered how power and hegemony might act against the promising future of trans self-publishing movements (Peters 2016d). Yet the hegemony was coming from inside the scene, as trans writers were already acknowledging in the form of critique. After all, trans self-publishing, zines, and DIY preexisted Topside and self-published novellas, as Cross noted. In the 2016 interview, Peters mentioned essayist, poet, and critic Jamie Berrout's work with self-publishing as "doing the same thing I'm doing," at least with respect to both of them sharing their work with other trans women online. However, Berrout was directly critiquing the scene of Topside for its continued failure to publish trans women of color writers, with the supposedly all-encompassing t4t potential of the scene in fact constituting a limited t4t. In 2016 Berrout published *Incomplete Short Stories and Essays*, which included detailed criticisms of Topside's absent or tokenizing attempts at inclusion while presenting a series of stories never finished, covering new ground while also standing as "a graveyard for trans stories that will never exist" (9–10). The assumption that trans work could start a new wave of trans literature was preventing an awareness that other trans writers could exist beyond its orbit—trans writers who live and write outside gentrified and gentrifying literary networks in Brooklyn, who did not want to be incorporated into its primarily white trans scene. Assumptive care was thus a part of the envisioned new age of trans literature, with its projection of t4t trying to grasp and claim ownership over what it did not hold.

What happened at the Topside Press Women's Writing Workshop, which was followed by its current status of still selling some books but largely letting them go out of print beyond Creative Commons, has become something of a hushed mystery when gestured to by those in the know. During a recent interview with Peters for her novel *Detransition, Baby*, interviewer Lila Shapiro attempted to find out what happened to Topside Press through an unnamed source. Shapiro (2021) reported that "the press had shut down because of infighting, disorganization, and financial strain. Writers of color criticized it for mostly publishing white women," while also including Peters's suggestion that it had become a "resented gatekeeper." There are elements of truth in all these, but they still take the appearance of double refraction, hushed and mostly anonymous while reducing "writers of color" to an amalgamation of divisive critique.

The truth, gestured toward by the *Vulture* interview, was that the dynamics of interpersonal conflict *and* abuse, skewed inclusion, and expulsion of critics or people who spoke out intensified as part of the scene of Topside even while it was a vision of t4t. Additionally, the workshop had mostly white attendees, did not adequately accommodate attendees with disabilities, and separated the two group subdivisions based on decisions about class and prestige.[1] The projection of a visionary trans lit scene that would inspire a new, unprecedented generation of trans writers, along with the difficulties of running a press, cast the ethos of t4t beyond its limited sphere and particular scene. Acknowledging such limits may also give us pause to accept Sarah Schulman's assertion in the *Vulture* interview that "there would be no Torrey without Topside," since clearly Peters's projects go beyond and outlast Topside, while this sentiment obscures that Peters was an important artist and interlocutor at the time of the press's existence (Shapiro 2021).

We can discuss short-circuited scenes of t4t in ways that are critical, sensitive, and blunt, diffusing some of the mystery around bygone scenes while airing "dirty laundry." Short-circuited scenes of trans cultural production are not new phenomena that have never been addressed. In "Hot Allostatic Load," for example, Porpentine Charity Heartscape (2015) wrote about the common abuse and disposal dynamics of feminist and trans cultural production scenes in the service of false ideals about "community." Heartscape further emphasized that these idealized deployments of "community" can be used to heighten emotional abuse in the scene, as the dissonance between the held-up ideology of community and what is actually happening can become disorienting and lead to self-blame. Thom's argument that abuse is commonplace and mishandled in queer and trans community also carries over into trans scenes of cultural production, even when those communities project and internalize an ethos of care and love such as t4t.

t4t as an idealized ethos risks making trans people feel crazy interpersonally and at the level of participation in cultural production. It risks producing a "we" that then gets imposed, glossing over the many wrongs trans people enact against each other. It risks covering over sexual harassment and assault, and it risks stifling dissent even as it claims to welcome dissent. It risks the irony of projecting care and community while disposing of trans people who are "divisive," perhaps even under the guise of protecting that person. It risks presenting a standpoint of marginalization that erases intracommunity marginalization and hierarchy. In so doing, t4t as cultural production produces the very dissent that it rejects while attempting to project an idealized, even if tumultuous, vision of community. Sitting with these risks laid bare is simply part of what it means to truly "know thy work."

A potential response, indicated by the discussion above, might be that t4t as an ethos already accommodates such fractures and failures, aware of its various bad feelings, hostilities, and tensions. I worry about the extent to which this absorption of negativity and difference can fuel dismissal, fatalism, or a blasé attitude toward situations of conflict or abuse that cannot be digested within a community. Furthermore, such an ethos of t4t may not explicitly attend to the ironic dynamics through which a projected community is used for assumptive care or exclusion. To explain some of these dynamics in more detail, I now move past the moment of Topside to discuss more recent ironies of professionalized trans literature scenes.

Trans Issues and the Prestige Economy

"We" might wonder, despite the failures produced by t4t in some scenes of cultural production, if something remains lost when trans cultural production gets instead taken up by mainstream, non-trans-run presses. When asked if trans literature is "entering a renaissance" in 2021, Schulman responded, "We might be leaving it" (Shapiro 2021). This is a curious use of "we," like many others, but worth some tempered consideration.

Trans literature reaching more mainstream heights through incorporation into mainstream presses and established nontrans small presses does not end the problem of a distorted "we." For example, Grace Lavery (2021) recently wrote a review of *Detransition, Baby*, introducing it as "the first great trans realist novel," somewhat deflated by a question mark. Of course, works by other trans realist novel writers exist, including Aoki's *He Mele a Hilo: A Hilo Song* in 2014, Thom's *Fierce Femmes and Notorious Liars* and Jia Qing Wilson-Yang's *Small Beauty* in 2016, Casey Plett's *Little Fish* in 2018, and Carter Sickels's *Prettiest Star* in 2020.[2] Without considering other trans realisms, one worries that getting proclaimed the first great trans book of whatever is based on the proximity of a book to the present and its perceived overall prestige.

There is more at stake here than bitterness about an understandably enthusiastic review. I worry about the phenomenon of declaring every few years a trans literature renaissance that jettisons previous trans writing in a revolving door of prestige while failing to support trans writers who do not fit the current moment. Heartscape (2015) mentions a similar phenomenon in "Hot Allostatic Load," writing,

> An entire industry of curation has sprung up to rigidly and sometimes violently police the hierarchy of who is allowed to express themselves as a trans or queer

person. The LGBT and queer spheres find it upon themselves to create compilations of the "best" art by trans people, to define what a trans story is and to omit the rest. Endless projects to curate, list, own, publish, control, but so few to offer support and mentorship.

Due to a lack of support and the wider cultural framing of trans people's lives as a consumable spectacle, trans cultural production risks relying on endless disconnected trans art moments built on a bottomless pit of discarded trans artists to exploit the demand for eternal trans novelty. People who cultivate an interest in trans art during any given "trans lit moment," even if trans, thus risk creating questionable canonizations and narratives around those canonizations (cf. Page 2021).

The issue of prestige and the composition of a "we" persists in trans cultural production. One repeated irony is the appeal to a stand-out trans "we" of cultural production that claims to be for "the trans community" but instead acts in the service of exclusion. In 2018 there was a call for a special trans issue of *Poetry Magazine*, after a report highlighted the lack of gender-nonconforming poets published in the magazine. The special issue was explicitly advertised as a means to foster trans inclusivity, framed as meeting "the need for an intentional community space," and planned for a release just before the Transgender Day of Remembrance (Soto 2017). Instead the project, which appointed a single curator of trans voices, effected a questionable exclusion. Rejections were sent out before the submission window for the issue officially closed, raising suspicions of a hasty or predetermined decision-making process, while the editor of the issue posted a comment on social media deriding several wide subjects of trans poetry as pedestrian (*Beyond Special Issue* 2018). In response to criticism from concerned trans poets, the special issue was silently removed.

Reflecting on the special issue, Yanyi (2018) linked its failure to a practice of care warped by the interplay of scarcity and commodification that shapes cultural production and poetry specifically. He wrote,

> Care, in a country where survival is tied to commerce, can be hijacked by commerce. The will to survive can disguise a will to profit. . . . Appointing a special-issues writer who speaks and edits for many means that there can be very few who rise to prominence, very few who reap the benefits beneath the institution's gleaming awnings, and very few contesting, discussing, and variegating the field of trans poetics with visibility.

As Yanyi argues, the special issue's call for trans inclusion in the name of community instead twisted care into commodification and exclusion under the mechanisms of professionalization and prestige.

In addition to curation, appeals to a questionable "we" can become a source for questionable critiques of trans art in the name of trans community. For example, in January 2020 Isabel Fall published a savvy speculative fiction story initially titled "I Sexually Identify as an Attack Helicopter," which flipped transphobic mockery on its head to critique the military industrial complex and the commodification of trans identity (Fall 2020). In addition to suspicions that the piece had been secretly penned by reactionaries, several trans people involved in science fiction literature scenes claimed that the story caused harm and invoked trauma against trans people to the extent that it should not have been published. These critiques were picked up by many nontrans authors involved in science fiction, several of them prestigious, to boost trans voices against the condemned trans story (Clark 2020). Ultimately the story was pulled by the author (Clarke 2020). Ironically, the appeal to a harmed trans "we" of trans science fiction, regardless of its accuracy or consensus, served to pulverize an emerging voice in trans science fiction. Care was a demand placed on Fall but not one reciprocated by her critics, who constructed a cohesive "we" as a means to exclude and expel.

As much as "we" might hope for a collective trans "we" and a worldmaking that can stand up to the profound lack of material support and hateful ideologies that stand against many trans lives, this hope must be tempered with some suspicion without reducing trans art to moments of disconnected prestige or genius, or to a tranquil refuge from challenge and bad feelings (see Billingsley 2015). *TSQ* itself, connected with an academy that presents trans scholars and their essays with the badge of their institutional affiliation, shares in these issues, even as it creates its own corridors to hold its critics (*TSQ*Now* 2020).

Trans people writing for other trans people is not over, regardless of the status of Topside or the incorporation of trans literature into mainstream literature. Though largely tethered to various prestige economies, unsupported, erased, or co-opted into the self-narratives of other scenes without support, trans writing persists in different modes. In addition to continuing her writing against the institutions of publishing, Berrout started a monthly booklet series publishing and paying trans women writers of color, which has now been passed on to the River Furnace collective (Wei Ling 2019; River Furnace n.d.). The continued life of trans publishing is thus not reducible to its "former" t4t scenes or contemporary successes of prestige in the publishing world or the academy (Berrout n.d.).

Conclusion: The T That Is a We and the T That Is an I

It is difficult to come back to even a tempered understanding of "community" after getting burned by interpersonal t4t or, as I have, t4t as it works its way into cultural production and even trans-queer bar-coffeeshop-restaurant-eventspacegourmetbakery-communitycenters. I worry that the preceding essay is both too mean and too kind. I open my copy of *The Masker* and see a sketch by Sybil Lamb of me, her, and Casey Plett hanging out in the city Plett eventually left, and that I now have left. I remember the Trans World-Making through Literature course I taught just before the workshop and its celebration of trans literature. I recall Thom's title of *I Hope We Choose Love.*

The vision of caring, contingent trans separatism offered by the ethos of t4t is not a complete lie, but it risks missing the ways that transphobia, misogyny, racism, and the effects of material scarcity carry over into these supposedly separatist spaces. Even a fully realized t4t sphere and its conflict would not be a horizontal field, since trans people can be so different from each other not only due to experience but also social status, exploitation, and access to institutions. Trans care thus seems to require some hesitation and caution against overreach, no longer fully separable from the many ways that care can become short-circuited between trans and cis people. There is much wisdom in t4t simply meaning sex, romance, and/or dating between trans people.

And yet there are several things that remain admirable to me in some of the intentions of t4t as ethos if not its realization: loving, connecting, discussing experiences that resonate, creating collaborative art, and sharing resources. I still enjoy when a friend expresses excitement about a particular t4t relationship or comes across trans art that speaks to them in ways they did not think were possible. I do not refuse to talk to people who continue to depend on the restaurant I worked at for social contact after I was laid off. I have almost finished reading *Detransition, Baby* and look forward to reading Jeanne Thornton's *Summer Fun,* Aoki's *Light from Uncommon Stars,* and Jackie Ess's finished version of *Darryl* later this year. t4t is thus exposed not as a totally false concept by this analysis but as one that often goes too far or can be used against the care it claims to foster. I hope this finds a way into the conversation about t4t and trans cultural production beyond getting dismissed as hostile or divisive.

Amy Marvin is a visiting assistant professor in philosophy at Gettysburg College. Her work can be found in *TSQ, Hypatia, Feminist Philosophy Quarterly,* the *APA Newsletter on LGBTQ Issues in Philosophy, Contingent Magazine, Curiosity Studies: Towards a New Ecology of Knowledge* (2020), and *We Want It All: An Anthology of Radical Trans Poetics* (2020). She was a coorganizer for the Trans* Experience in Philosophy Conference in 2016.

Acknowledgments
I thank Isobel Bess for her feedback, Jackie Ess for her hospitality, the reviewers, Topside Press for covering my travel, and Rocío Zambrana for her reading of Hegel.

Notes

1.   I was an attendee at the workshop who stayed with another attendee, and I have discussed the workshop with other attendees over the following years. Though this essay may at times come across with the tone of an insider, I traveled to the workshop as an outsider full of hope for t4t and related trans lit projects. Just before the workshop I taught a course titled Trans World-Making through Literature in celebration of the Topside scene, and much of this essay and its citations are a partial palinode for this syllabus in light of subsequently witnessing that scene fall apart, among other events. As a critic I am thus both retrospective and complicit in the aspirations of these scenes, even as my access was somewhat fragmented, much like the reconstruction I now present to the reader.

2.   One objection, raised by a reviewer, is that *Fierce Femmes and Notorious Liars* does not qualify as a trans realist novel. These types of objections lead to questions about what counts as trans realism, whether or not trans magical realism is a form of trans realism, and to what extent these taxonomies are helpful or unhelpful for trans literature. Whether or not my list is correct, this is the type of rich discussion that gets overlooked by proclaiming a recent, popular book the first great trans such-and-such.

References

Aoki, Ryka. 2014. "Ryka Aoki." Interview by Nia King. In *Queer and Trans Artists of Color: Stories of Some of Our Lives*, 1–16. Self-published.

Awkward-Rich, Cameron. 2020. "t4t: Toward a Crip Ethics of Trans Literary Criticism." In *The Routledge Companion to Literature and Disability*, edited by Alice Hall, 31–42. New York: Routledge.

Berrout, Jamie. n.d. "Support." www.jamieberrout.com/support (accessed September 25, 2021).

Berrout, Jamie. 2016. *Incomplete Short Stories and Essays*. Gumroad. gumroad.com/jamieberrout (accessed January 12, 2021). Page numbers from the original version that was taken offline. Excerpts available in *Nat. Brut*, no. 11. www.natbrut.com/jamie-berrout.

Beyond Special Issue. 2018. Statements by Chase Berggrun, Jos Charles, jayy dodd, Kam Hilliard, TC Tolbert, and Candace Williams. Tumblr. beyondspecialissue.tumblr.com.

Billingsley, Amy. 2015. "Hope in a Vice: Carole Pateman, Judith Butler, and Suspicious Hope." *Hypatia* 30, no. 3: 597–612.

Binnie, Imogen. 2013a. "Dan Fishback Interviews Imogen Binnie." Interview by Dan Fishback. Emily Books, July 28. emilybooks.com/2013/07/28/dan-fishback-interviews-imogen-binnie/.

Binnie, Imogen. 2013b. *Nevada*. New York: Topside.

Butler, Judith. 1995. "Contingent Foundations." In *Feminist Contentions: A Philosophical Exchange*, edited by Seyla Benhabib, Judith Butler, Drucilla Cornell, and Nancy Fraser, 35–58. New York: Routledge.

Clark, M. L. 2020. "How an Experimental Story about Gender and Warfare Shook the Sci-Fi Community." *Verge*, January 22. www.theverge.com/2020/1/22/21076981/isabel-fall-clarkesworld-attack-helicopter-short-story-gender-art-controversy.

Clarke, Neil. 2020. "About the Story by Isabel Fall." *Clarkesworld*, no. 160. clarkesworldmagazine.com/fall_01_20/.

Cross, Katherine. 2014. "Know and Tell: The Literary Renaissance of Trans Women Writers. *Bitch Magazine*, November 21. www.bitchmedia.org/article/trans-women-literary-fiction-renaissance.

Fall, Isabel. 2020. "I Sexually Identify as an Attack Helicopter." *Clarkesworld*, no. 160. Removed from the internet.

Heartscape, Porpentine Charity. 2015. "Hot Allostatic Load." *New Inquiry*, May 11. thenewinquiry
.com/hot-allostatic-load/.

Lavery, Grace. 2021. "*Detransition, Baby* by Torrey Peters. Review—A Comedy of Manners."
Guardian, January 7. www.theguardian.com/books/2021/jan/07/detransition-baby-by
-torrey-peters-review-a-comedy-of-manners.

Léger, Tom. 2012. "Know Thy Work: A Note from the Publisher." In *The Collection: Short Fiction
from the Transgender Vanguard*, edited by Tom Léger and Riley MacLeod, 389–92. New
York: Topside.

Léger, Tom, and Riley MacLeod. 2012. Introduction to *The Collection: Short Fiction from the
Transgender Vanguard*, edited by Tom Léger and Riley MacLeod, 1–3. New York: Topside.

Léger, Tom, and Riley MacLeod. 2013. *Is There a Transgender Text in This Class? A Zine about
Teaching Trans Fiction and Poetry*. New York: Topside.

Malatino, Hil. 2019. "Future Fatigue: Trans Intimacies and Trans Presents (or How to Survive the
Interregnum)." *TSQ* 6, no. 4: 635–58.

Malatino, Hil. 2020. *Trans Care*. Minneapolis: University of Minnesota Press.

Marvin, Amy. 2019. "Assumptive Care and Futurebound Care in Trans Literature." *APA Newsletter on LGBTQ Issues in Philosophy* 19, no. 1. cdn.ymaws.com/www.apaonline.org
/resource/collection/B4B9E534-A677-4F29-8DC9-D75A5F16CC55/LGBTQV19n1.pdf.

Namaste, Viviane. 2019. "Undoing Theory: The 'Transgender Question' and the Epistemic Violence of Anglo-American Feminist Theory." *Hypatia* 24, no. 3: 11–32.

Page, Morgan M. 2021. "Never Be New Again." Substack, January 19. valleyofthed.substack.com/p
/never-be-new-again.

Peters, Torrey. 2016a. *Infect Your Friends and Loved Ones*. www.torreypeters.com/book/infect
-your-friends-and-loved-ones/.

Peters, Torrey. 2016b. *Masker*. Self-published. www.torreypeters.com/book/the-masker/.

Peters, Torrey. 2016c. "T4T: Trans Author Torrey Peters on Sisterhood and Taboo." Interview by
Danielle Rose. *Wussy Mag*, December 9. www.wussymag.com/all/2016/12/9/t4t-trans
-author-torrey-peters-on-sisterhood-and-taboo.

Peters, Torrey. 2016d. "Torrey Peters." Interview by Merritt Kopas. *Woodland Secrets*, episode 60,
June 11. Audio recording. woodlandsecrets.co/episode/60.

Peters, Torrey. 2017. "(Trans) Love and Other Scars: An Interview with Torrey Peters, Author of
Infect Your Friends and Loved Ones." Interview by Kai Cheng Thom. *Autostraddle*, February 20. www.autostraddle.com/trans-love-and-other-scars-an-interview-with-torrey
-peters-author-of-infect-your-friends-and-loved-ones-369764/.

Peters, Torrey. 2021. "Writing for a Trans Audience: Talking with Torrey Peters." Interview by
Carter Sickels. *Rumpus*, January 18. therumpus.net/2021/01/the-rumpus-interview-with
-torrey-peters/.

Peters, Torrey, and Clutch Fleischmann. 2016. "T Clutch Fleischmann and Torrey Peters on Trans
Essays." *Essay Daily*, January 4. www.essaydaily.org/2016/01/t-clutch-fleischmann-and
-torrey-peters.html.

Plett, Casey. 2015. "Rise of the Gender Novel." *Walrus*, March 18. Updated April 10, 2020. thewalrus
.ca/rise-of-the-gender-novel/.

River Furnace. n.d. Patreon page. www.patreon.com/transwomenwriters (accessed January 12,
2020).

Ross, Mirha-Soleil, and Xanthra Phillippa, dirs. 1993. *Gender Troublemakers*. Film. Toronto:
V-Tape.

Shapiro, Lila. 2021. "Torrey Peters Goes There." Interview with Torrey Peters. *Vulture*, January 6. www.vulture.com/2021/01/torrey-peters-detransition-baby.html.

Soto, Christopher. 2017. "'Poetry' Magazine Will Feature Trans/GNC Poets in Special Issue." *Lambda Literary*, October 31. www.lambdaliterary.org/2017/10/poetry-magazine-will -feature-trans-poets/.

Thom, Kai Cheng. 2019. *I Hope We Choose Love: A Trans Girl's Notes from the End of the World.* Vancouver, BC: Arsenal Pulp.

*TSQ*Now*. 2020. Transamory Cluster. www.tsqnow.online/blog/categories/transamory-cluster.

Valens, Ana. 2016. "This Is Why I Write: Almost All Stories about Trans Women Are Written by Cisgender Authors." *Bitch Magazine*, August 4. www.bitchmedia.org/article/why-i-write -almost-all-stories-about-trans-women-are-written-cisgender-authors.

Wei Ling, Tony. 2019. "Speculative-Speculative Fiction: Jamie Berrout's Impossible Trans Literatures." UCLA: Center for the Study of Women Blog, March 15. csw.ucla.edu/2019/03 /05/speculative-speculative-fiction-jamie-berrouts-impossible-trans-literatures/.

Williams, Rachel Anne. 2019. *Transgressive: A Trans Woman on Gender, Feminism, and Politics.* London: Jessica Kingsley.

Yanyi. 2018. "Counting Tokens: Special Issues and the Theatre of Delay." Asian American Writers' Workshop, August 19. aaww.org/counting-tokens-special-issues/.

The Affective Politics of Care in Trans Crowdfunding

CHRIS BARCELOS

Abstract Trans-for-trans crowdfunding is a common strategy to raise money both for gender-affirming medical care and for survival expenses related to living in a transphobic world. Although crowdfunding is infrequently successful in funding our survival needs, there have been few attempts to theorize what this form of mutual aid accomplishes. The objective of this article is to explore the possibilities and limits of trans crowdfunding as part of a critical trans political project. Drawing on the emergent body of scholarship in trans care and the cultural sites in which t4t crowdfunding circulates, this article asks: how does thinking about trans crowdfunding as an affect, labor, and politics of care help us understand its utility, even in the face of its failures to redistribute wealth and meet our material needs? The author argues that trans crowdfunding functions as a form of "complicit care" that simultaneously furthers both our marginalization and our collective liberation.
Keywords crowdfunding, care labor, care politics, affect, t4t

Like most trans people, my social media feeds are filled with urgent requests from other trans folks to crowdfund their healthcare, housing, and other survival needs. I often find myself scrolling past a seemingly endless collection of crowdfunding campaigns for gender-affirming medical care expenses. Even before the COVID-19 crisis, these medical campaigns were interspersed with requests to fund material day-to-day needs—food, clothing, shelter—as well as nonmaterial, affective needs such as crowdsourcing help to navigate the systems that gatekeep the things we need. I regularly feel a rising sense of irritation as I click through campaign after campaign. I feel resentful that our well-being is subject to a popularity contest in which those who craft the most compelling story and are the most social media savvy are more likely to get (some of) their needs met. I am angry that trans people cannot simply get the care they need to thrive. I am also irritated at what feels like a nonstop parade of young, white, trans masculine folks raising money for chest surgery in states that mandate trans-inclusive healthcare coverage—I'm irritated that the most privileged among us seem to feel the most entitled to our scarce financial resources.

TSQ: Transgender Studies Quarterly ★ Volume 9, Number 1 ★ February 2022
DOI 10.1215/23289252-9475495   © 2022 Duke University Press

What began as a feeling of unease about intracommunity trans politics surrounding this particular form of mutual aid transformed into a research project. I used GoFundMe.com to collect 410 trans crowdfunding campaigns for gender-affirming care that were created from March 2012 to May 2016 across six countries. I then analyzed the financial success of each campaign, the recipient demographics, and the narrative strategies used to elicit donations (Barcelos 2019; Barcelos and Budge 2019; Barcelos 2020). At the time I conducted this research, few scholars and activists had written about the practice and politics of crowdfunding in trans communities.[1] The data confirmed my suspicions about trans crowdfunding: the majority of campaigns were to benefit young, white, trans masculine people raising money for gender-affirming chest surgery. Transgender men constituted 70 percent of recipients, and campaigns for masculinizing chest surgery overall accounted for 62 percent of campaigns. Trans people of color represented only 13 percent of total recipients. Although recipients ranged in age from fifteen to seventy-three, the average age was twenty-four. Across all campaigns, very few recipients reached their goals, and most did not even come close—on average campaigns only raised 24 percent of their goal. There were also clear gender differences; even when taking into account the influence of Facebook shares and number of Facebook friends, trans men overall raised more money and a higher percentage of their goal than trans women.

This research demonstrated an important and rarely discussed aspect of trans crowdfunding: its capacity not only to reveal but also to reproduce inequalities. To be sure, trans communities know that our need to crowdfund is a response to inequality. Many of us turn to crowdfunding when our insurance plan refuses to pay for our healthcare, when we can't make rent because we were fired by a transphobic supervisor, or when we need emergency housing to escape from an abusive family of origin. For better or worse, trans communities know that we must rely on crowdfunding to make our lives livable in the face of historic and ongoing state violence. As a practice of mutual aid, crowdfunding is a strategy to "meet each other's basic survival needs with a shared understanding that the systems we live under are not going to meet our needs" (Spade 2020a). Yet crowdfunding in trans communities also reproduces many of the same inequities that it is a response to: stratifications of deservingness and merit, white supremacy, adherence to gender normativity, transmisogyny, and so on (Barcelos 2019; Barcelos 2020; King 2013). In my analysis of trans medical crowdfunding, recipients' campaign narratives both reflected and reproduced discourses of deservingness, neoliberal notions of personal responsibility, and medicalized transnormativity (Barcelos 2019). In other words, despite its redistributive aims, crowdfunding is also complicit in the conditions of oppression.

The landscape of trans crowdfunding has changed quite a bit in the few years since I conducted this research. First, although web-based medical crowd-funding in trans communities continues unabated, there has been a shift to other types of platforms, notably direct transfers via apps like Venmo and CashApp. Similarly, at least pre-COVID-19, there seemed to be a resurgence of in-person fundraisers at bars, performance venues, and collective spaces. Second, the schol-arly literature on crowdfunding has grown considerably, though this growth has focused primarily on crowdfunding outside trans communities. The findings in this work are remarkably consistent and reinforce my own: crowdfunding is financially successful for very few people, and those who are successful at crowd-funding tend to have preexisting resources and privileges (Kenworthy et al. 2020; Berliner and Kenworthy 2017; Kimseylove, Edwards, and Inwards-Breland 2020). This research almost exclusively uses empirical social science methodologies, and few scholars have analyzed t4t crowdfunding as a cultural text.[2] Third, the COVID-19 crisis has amplified the visibility and popularity of mutual aid prac-tices in the face of exponentially increased precarity around the world. Pre-viously a practice associated with leftist social movements, mutual aid is becom-ing a household term at risk of being co-opted into the very structures of racial capitalism that it seeks to work against (Spade 2020a). Last, and importantly, uprisings in the summer of 2020 following the police murders of George Floyd, Breonna Taylor, Tony McDade, and countless others contributed to an out-pouring of donations to mutual aid projects and direct cash transfers to Black trans people and Black trans-led organizations (Anderson 2020; Nowell 2020).

Amid all of these shifts, we have yet to adequately theorize the politics and practice of trans-for-trans crowdfunding. Anecdotally, trans folks know that crowdfunding is an enduring feature of our communities. Empirically, we've seen that crowdfunding rarely succeeds in meeting our needs for surgery, rent, or cre-ative projects. What, then, does trans crowdfunding accomplish, given that it does not fulfill its ostensible purpose of funding material survival needs? Put another way, what does crowdfunding "do" for us? In what follows, I build on my previous work analyzing medical crowdfunding campaigns by examining a broad archive of the sites where t4t crowdfunding circulates, including medical crowdfunding but also direct cash transfers and mutual aid projects. I use this emerging archive as a basis from which to theorize the politics of care in t4t crowdfunding and to offer generative provocations on its possibilities and limits in terms of trans liber-ation. In weaving together research on crowdfunding inequalities, cultural arti-facts from t4t crowdfunding, and theorizing in trans care (Malatino 2020; Hwang 2019; Marvin 2019; Machuca Rose 2019; Malatino 2019; Aizura 2017), this analy-sis responds to Hil Malatino's (2020: 68) call for "a dual movement wherein we highlight the imperfection and complicity that characterizes contemporary forms of trans care praxis as we push for collective redistribution." Alongside Malatino, I argue that we need to interrogate the constraints on trans-for-trans mutual aid practices such as crowdfunding in order to "call attention to the epistemologies, systems, and technologies that contribute to such unjust apportioning, even as we must navigate them in order to get (some of) our needs met" (68). In short, how does thinking about trans crowdfunding as care work help us understand its utility, even in the face of its failure to redistribute wealth or adequately meet our material needs? What forms of inequality emerge in trans crowdfunding as affective care labor?

I argue that t4t crowdfunding functions as a form of "complicit care" that simultaneously furthers both our marginalization and our collective liberation. As an individual-level solution to structural-level problems, crowdfunding as complicit care colludes in maintaining structural violence. Crowdfunding distributes feelings *of* care (and being cared *for*) that more often than not mirror logics of white supremacy, transnormativity, and neoliberalism. Nonetheless, trans crowdfunding is also care labor in the form of a "t4t praxis of love," a small act that makes life more livable in the spaces between now and our collective liberation (Malatino 2019). After considering crowdfunding in relation to the practice and politics of mutual aid, I look to archives of t4t crowdfunding to analyze how the practice is at once an affect, politics, and labor of trans care (Puig de la Bellacasa 2017). As a provocation for future inquiry, I argue that t4t crowdfunding is best understood as a form of affective labor, rather than effective material wealth redistribution.

Situating Crowdfunding as an Imperfect Practice of Mutual Aid

The struggle to meet basic survival needs under racial capitalism created—and proliferated—the rise of crowdfunding in marginalized communities. Although the lack of universal healthcare in the United States means that even people with racial, economic, and gender privilege must turn to crowdfunding to cover out-of-pocket expenses (Kenworthy et al. 2020), crowdfunding is particularly endemic to communities fighting to survive in the face of necropolitical and state neglect. Crowdfunding falls under the umbrella term *crowdsourcing*, which simply means turning to social networks to meet financial, material, and affective needs. The ubiquitous medical crowdfunding campaign on GoFundMe.com is only one example of how trans communities practice mutual aid as a form of solidarity. The general and particular forms of social and economic exclusion faced by trans people, and especially multiply minoritized trans communities, have forced us to hone our craft of getting needs met both within and beyond existing structures. In organized and spontaneous fashion, trans communities provide financial, emotional, logistical, and political support to one another: buddy systems for accompaniment to medical appointments to protect against incompetent care; fundraisers for survival expenses following a transphobic attack on the street; collective housing arrangements; and crowdsourced lists of trans-friendly therapists, electrolysists, and barbers.

Crowdfunding can be a practice of mutual aid, yet it is distinct in several important aspects that highlight its limitations as part of the political project of trans liberation. In Dean Spade's (2020a: 18) definition, mutual aid is "collective coordination to meet each other's needs, usually [starting] from an awareness that the systems we have in place are not going to meet them." Mutual aid has a rich history in liberation movements, both in response to the ongoing conditions of white supremacy, settler colonialism, and racial capitalism that contribute to "slow deaths" (Berlant 2007), as well as in response to the acute crises of "natural" disasters like hurricanes, wildfires, and infectious disease pandemics. Among the more well-known examples of mutual aid projects in liberation movements are the Black Panther Party's food and healthcare programs such as free breakfasts and medical clinics (Nelson 2011; Hilliard 2008). These programs combined the provision of basic needs with political education—a strategy of survival pending the revolution and a "model for all oppressed people who wish to begin to take concrete actions to deal with their oppression" (Hilliard 2008: 3). Tamara Kneese (2020) notes that a "core tenet of mutual aid is drawing support from within communities instead of relying on external charitable actions, which are often tied to colonialist and paternalistic rhetorics of development." In contrast, "crowdfunding relies on neoliberal notions of charitable giving and the responsibility of moral individuals," and therefore Kneese argues that it is not a form of mutual aid.

The COVID-19 crisis brought renewed attention to mutual aid, and along with it the potential to water down its revolutionary potential. In the winter and spring of 2020, *mutual aid* seemed to become a household term, with hundreds of new mutual aid groups popping up across the United States and around the world (Ortega and Orsini 2020; Ticktin 2020). However, this popularity runs the risk of reducing mutual aid to just another form of charity, one that mirrors the depoliticized objectives and priorities of nonprofit organizations, elite donors, and others invested in benevolent white supremacy (Chua 2020; Kouri-Towe 2020). Spade offers three key elements of mutual aid projects, which I slightly alter here to think about t4t mutual aid. According to Spade (2020b), mutual aid projects 1) work to meet trans people's survival needs and build shared understanding about why trans folks do not have what they need to survive; 2) mobilize trans people, expand trans solidarity, and build trans liberation movements; and 3) are participatory forms of action in which trans people solve our problems through collective action rather than waiting for help. Viewed through this framework, most t4t crowdfunding meets only the first part of element 1: it attempts to meet our survival needs, albeit only partially. For the most part, t4t crowdfunding does not mobilize an analysis of why we don't have what we need to survive and occurs in isolation from larger solidarity movements and forms of collective action. As I argue in this article, understanding the affective dimensions of t4t crowdfunding as acts of trans solidarity and care is a strategy to understand crowdfunding's limitations.

Compared to other forms of mutual aid, we know more about how web-based medical crowdfunding fails to meet our survival needs. Beginning in the mid-2010s, a growing body of research has investigated how medical crowd-funding online is both a response to and a driver of the maldistribution of healthcare resources. First, medical crowdfunding campaigns are a Band-aid on the vast inequities of the US healthcare system, in which millions of people remain uninsured or underinsured despite the Affordable Care Act. Likewise, the legacy of the medical model of transsexualism (Gill-Peterson 2018) that contributed to gender-affirming care's being seen as "elective," along with rollbacks of pro-tections for trans-inclusive care under the Trump regime, have fueled the need for trans people to turn to their social networks to fund their care. As one indica-tion of the scope of medical crowdfunding, users on GoFundMe.com raise over $650 million a year for healthcare expenses (GoFundMe 2020b). Second, medical crowdfunding campaigns very rarely reach their goal; analyses have found that campaigns on average raise about only 40 percent of their goal (Kenworthy et al. 2020; Berliner and Kenworthy 2017). In my research on trans crowdfunding for gender-affirming care, that number was, even lower, at about 24 percent of the goal (Barcelos 2020). Third, there are significant racial inequities in medical crowdfunding. In my work, 87 percent of campaigns were for white trans recip-ients, and in Nora Kenworthy and colleagues' (2020) general analysis,[3] 77 percent of campaigns were for white recipients—evidence that trans medical crowd-funding is even whiter than crowdfunding overall. This research also found that being Black was associated with earning $22 less per donation compared to white recipients, even when the size of one's online social network was taken into account. Additionally, both my research and that focused on non-trans crowd-funding reveal how the strategic narratives used in campaigns mobilize neoliberal understandings of deservingness. Crowdfunding is an individual-level solution to structural problems in which having a "worthy," well-crafted story is the arbiter of receiving care (Berliner and Kenworthy 2017; Barcelos 2019; Kneese 2020).

Sites of t4t Crowdfunding

To theorize the politics of care in t4t crowdfunding, I explore four sites through which it circulates: the ubiquitous GoFundMe surgery campaign, direct cash transfers via apps like CashApp and Venmo, the outpouring of contributions to

Black trans organizations and individuals following uprisings in the summer of 2020, and a holiday project called "Trans Santa." This is not an exhaustive archive; rather, it is a selection of salient, highly visible, and growing sites in which t4t crowdfunding occurs. Although it is almost impossible to measure what proportion of donations to a trans person's crowdfunding campaign is from other trans people, anecdotally, it is safe to say that trans people are overrepresented as donors in each other's campaigns as an act of t4t solidarity and care. I use this brief survey of the trans crowdfunding archive to demonstrate how feeling, inequality, and care labor travel through t4t crowdfunding in the form of "complicit care."

The Ubiquitous GoFundMe Medical Campaign

Typing *transgender* into the search bar on GoFundMe.com results in over ten thousand campaigns, most of them for gender-affirming medical care. The site algorithm shows you the more financially successful campaigns first, lending potential users a false sense of the likelihood that they could fulfill their needs by fundraising on the site. Indeed, this is part of the website's business model, in which they have fashioned themselves as a solution to the nonexistent safety net in the United States (GoFundMe 2020c). The site cheerfully states that their service can "help others overcome hardship and meet aspirational goals" with the help of their "Customer Happiness Agents" and tutorials on how to craft a compelling campaign narrative. In trans social media networks, a less sanguine set of campaigns circulate. A nonbinary South Asian person on a trans feminine spectrum struggles to meet a high goal for an undisclosed set of gender-affirming procedures. The recipient has been effectively unemployed since the beginning of the COVID-19 crisis. Both the recipient and other trans people in our overlapping social networks share the campaign regularly, but it seldom inches toward its goal. A mixed-race, Black trans masculine nonbinary person slowly creeps toward their goal of affording gender-affirming top surgery. Despite having a full-time job and employer-based health insurance, they live in a state that statutorily eliminated trans-inclusive care. The campaign narrative articulates all of this in the context of how the state does violence toward trans bodies, particularly trans bodies of color. In the photo, the recipient holds a hand-drawn sign that reads, "trans people exist because our ancestors existed."

Direct Cash Transfers via Apps

"Urgent," reads the Instagram story, "Black trans femme needs help getting back on her feet!!," along with a list of her CashApp, Venmo, and PayPal links. This story is reshared by practically every trans person in my friends list. There is no way of knowing how many of them sent the recipient money, and most of them were underemployed even before the COVID-19 crisis. Over on Facebook, things are a bit more organized, with specific groups set up for people to share their calls for support. My local groups, Boston Trans Exchange and Boston Queers for Mutual Aid, have specific posting guidelines for users seeking direct cash transfers. The latter explains, "This group was created as a space for radical queer and trans folks to sell things, crowdsource information, request help, find housing, share resources, etc." (Boston Queers for Mutual Aid 2021). Posts for financial assistance via CashApp or Venmo must follow a particular format that includes the goal amount, current amount raised, where else the request was cross-posted, and an edit when/if the goal is met. In the trans-only group, users can post no more than once per week, and all requests together cannot exceed $1,000 per month. Rent and medical needs are exempted from these rules. Requests from these groups are prominent on my time line, and for the most part they are desperate appeals to fund basic survival needs—food, transportation, housing, and gender-affirming clothing. Nearly all posts go unfunded, and the majority of the comments are "bumps" or cute animal pictures attempting to skirt the algorithm that Facebook purportedly uses to demote individual user crowdfunding posts.

Funding Black Trans Life
In the summer of 2020, in the midst of the ongoing COVID-19 crisis and following the police murder of George Floyd, Black-led organizations in the United States experienced a deluge of financial donations. In the immediate wake of Floyd's murder by the Minneapolis police, local nonprofits and bail funds received such an overwhelming amount of donations that they began using their social media platforms to redirect potential donors to other Black-led organizations (Anderson, 2020). Black trans-led projects and organizations capitalized on this outpouring of solidarity and the not-insignificant element of complacent white guilt that may have prompted these donations. For instance, in early June the New York City–based organization GLITS (Gays and Lesbians Living in a Transgender Society), headed by Ceyenne Doroshow, raised over $1 million USD in about a week. This unprecedented—and unexpected—outpouring enabled Doroshow to purchase an eleven-unit building in Queens, as she told *Teen Vogue*, a dream she'd had for thirty years (Nowell 2020). In the tradition of Sylvia Rivera and Marsha P. Johnson's short-lived STAR House, the GLITS residence will provide housing, community, and political education for queer and trans people facing housing insecurity—but this time the building is owned by a Black trans woman community leader. Similar fundraising efforts during the early months of the COVID-19 crisis witnessed notable sums of money raised for BIPOC queer and trans communities. In March 2020 a team of organizers used GoFundMe to raise over

$250,000 USD for the "COVID-19 Mutual Aid Fund for LGBTQI+ BIPOC Folks" (GoFundMe 2020a). These funds were distributed through a "rolling jubilee" based on specific criteria to prioritize the most vulnerable. The fund distributed $100 each to about two-thirds of recipients, and an average of $147 to the remaining third. Similarly, in April 2020 Indya Moore raised over $20,000 USD via posts on Instagram, which the *Pose* star then redistributed in $50 increments via CashApp to Black queer and trans folks who direct messaged them or posted in the comments (Street 2020b).

Trans Santa

Moore also launched Trans Santa in late 2020, a crowdsourced holiday gift-giving project in which trans youth under age twenty-four submitted a hand-drawn "wish list" that was posted to Instagram and linked to a Target registry. This setup enabled anyone on the internet to anonymously send gifts to young trans people; many of the letters to Santa also included the recipient's CashApp or Venmo links. The goal of the campaign was to "show young trans people that they are loved, supported, and have a family around the country and the world of people who will care for them during the holidays" (Street 2020a). By Christmas Day, Trans Santa had 935 wish lists, with the majority of them having received at least some of the presents requested. The collection of colorful wish lists posted on the project's Instagram feed underscored the need for the project and laid bare the conditions of precarity and marginalization faced by trans youth. Although there were certainly requests for traditional holiday gifts such as video games and other consumer electronics, an overwhelming number of wish lists asked for basic survival items: food, toiletries, cleaning supplies, and other household goods. Many lists asked for gender-affirming clothing and personal care items, material goods that transphobic parents had denied their children. A great number of wish lists painfully detailed how rejection from parents or guardians meant that they were unable to receive the gendered gifts that mattered to them. Even youth who wrote letters stating that they had a supportive family frequently mentioned that pandemic-related economic precarity meant that they could not afford any holiday gifts.

Trans Crowdfunding as a Politics of Affective Care Labor

This archive of t4t crowdfunding demonstrates the urgent demand to meet trans people's material and affective survival needs. It also highlights the necessity to think capaciously about the limits and possibilities of crowdfunding as part of a critical trans political project. In many ways, crowdfunding is a practice of "putting Band-aids on bullet holes" that redistributes the burden of inequality onto marginalized communities. Essentially, we are passing around the same $20, attempting to fix problems that we did not create (Kenworthy 2019): housing insecurity, lack of healthcare access, and transphobic violence. Like all archives, this collection of t4t crowdfunding is partial and messy; I use it to offer provocations about what t4t crowdfunding accomplishes, given that it insufficiently meets our material needs, and even when it does, it is not usually part of a larger, sustainable project of trans liberation. Putting this archive in conversation with the literature on trans care is a strategy to theorize what the practice "does" in trans communities. Future empirical work could demonstrate the distribution and determinants of inequalities in t4t crowdfunding, for instance, how often funding requests by trans women of color are shared by white trans masculine people, and to what success.

Scholarship on queer and trans care has emerged in response to the need to situate care labor and care ethics outside cisgender, heteronormative, white, middle-class family formations (Manalansan 2008). In transing and queering the tradition of feminist care ethics, trans care reconfigures a "situated, trans, ethical wisdom of care that links dependency with solidarity in particular communities" (Marvin 2019: 105). At the center of transing care is a desire to imagine a relational praxis of care that cuts across material and affective registers. Writing about the strategies of survival that transverse carceral spaces, Ren-yo Hwang (2019: 564) invokes a relational practice of "deviant care" that "require[s] us to question short-term fixes, particularly ones that seek to decontextualize material and historical power relations that moderate the possibility for social change." Similarly, what Elijah Adiv Edelman (2020: 112) terms "trans vitalities" reject the neoliberal impulse behind concepts like "resilience" to instead center an ethics of radical care that disrupts and rethinks "what valuable, viable, or quantifiable quality of life looks like." There is also a need to reconceptualize the neoliberalization and co-optation of "self-care" as a strategy not to fulfill the needs of capital but instead to achieve a revolutionary praxis in which care of the self is, in Audre Lorde's (1988: 130) famous words, "an act of political warfare." James McMaster (2020: 184) uses the work of trans feminine Filipinx/a artist Mark Aguhar to make this point: "The care of the self can be a politically urgent performance through which minoritarian subjects might fashion themselves more pleasurable, livable lives." Indeed, as Malatino (2020) notes, fashioning these livable lives is a relational praxis that serves necessary affective ends. Writing about his experience of scrolling through trans crowdfunding campaigns on social media (as I opened this essay), Malatino admits, "Sometimes, I can throw money at these requests. Sometimes, the most I can do is commiserate in frustrated empathy. Both of these responses are trans care praxis" (64). In this sense, trans crowdfunding invokes an affect of trans care solidarity—we may not be able to meet other trans people's material needs, but we can share our feelings of commiseration, empathy, and care alongside small donations or resharing crowdfunding requests.

Thinking about trans crowdfunding as simultaneously an affect, politics, and labor of care (Puig de la Bellacasa 2017) helps us understand its utility in the face of its failure to effectively redistribute wealth and meet our material survival needs. Even in the inability to throw money at these requests, as Malatino describes, there is a relational act of care that extends beyond the ability to finance surgery or housing. The small amounts of money circulating through t4t Venmo transactions attest to these acts of care—despite lacking the financial wealth to redistribute notable sums of money, directly sending $5 or $10 to fund another trans person's housing or healthcare is a relational practice that signals care and solidarity in the face of oppressive systems. Anonymously buying holiday presents for trans youth is a similar act of care that centers trans kids' joy and pleasure—giving them roses while they're still here (Tandy 2015)—rather than focusing solely on their dispro-portionate poor mental health or suicide rates (Bochicchio et al. 2021). Similarly, the labor of care involved in carrying out or contributing to mutual aid projects such as the GLITS house or COVID-19 relief invokes a relational care praxis in trans communities that centers those multiply marginalized by interlocking sys-tems of oppression. In other words, despite the often scarce resources in trans communities that limit significant material redistribution, there is an abundance of affective resources. As Aren Aizura and Malatino (2019) put it, we care a lot. Sending a small sum for bus money via Venmo or buying a holiday gift for a trans youth may not fundamentally alter the conditions of social marginalization and exclusion, but it does represent a labor of caregiving, a feeling of belonging and solidarity, and an investment in a form of trans politics that links solidarity and dependency (Marvin 2019).

Despite its work as act of care, we might think of t4t crowdfunding as a form of "complicit care" that works both for and against our liberation. As an individual-level solution to structural-level problems, it is complicit in the neo-liberal politics that shifts the burden of inequality onto marginalized people. As with crowdfunding more generally, t4t crowdfunding privatizes responsibility for ameliorating the conditions of racial capitalism (Berliner and Kenworthy 2017). In the context of the overall economic marginalization of trans people, one broke trans person who receives $20 to buy groceries through sharing their Venmo on social media, and is later able to contribute $20 to a medical fundraiser, is an example of individualizing the burden of economic inequality. This is especially so when the money often circulates in a fashion divorced from a broader political analysis, one that is absent from most medical crowdfunding campaigns or direct cash transfer requests. As the COVID-19 crisis has made abundantly clear, crowd-funded financial redistribution alone cannot obviate the suffering caused by disaster capitalism and necropolitical state neglect. As important as the $100 or so that people received from crowdfunded COVID-19 mutual aid relief efforts may have been, it certainly was not enough to sustain anyone for long in the absence of meaningful government income assistance or eviction protection. As important as receiving gender-affirming gifts from Trans Santa may have been for a young trans person, these gifts cannot prevent transphobic parents from kicking their children out of the home or prevent state legislatures from attempting to outlaw gender-affirming medical care for youth. Naming the complicity of trans crowdfunding does not discount the importance of these efforts in terms of their ability to provide affective care and demonstrate trans political solidarity. Instead, I offer the provocation that t4t crowdfunding is more successful as an affective care practice than a wealth redistribution effort, as an invitation to think carefully about what it can and cannot do for our collective liberation.

Although trans crowdfunding may perform a relational care ethic, like other forms of caregiving labor, it is nonetheless complicit in the reproduction of gendered inequalities (Aizura 2020; Ward 2010) and hierarchies of deservingness (Barcelos 2019). As Kenworthy and colleagues (2020) point out in their analysis of cisgender medical crowdfunding, women are much more likely to take on the feminized caring labor of running crowdfunding campaigns, thus constituting a new form of digital care labor. Likewise, feminist scholars of affect in digital media have emphasized that feminized, unpaid labor relies on selfless "caring" and "compassion" to serve the needs of capital (Duffy 2016; Jarrett 2014). Notably, the archive of t4t crowdfunding reveals that trans women and femmes are overrepresented in trans digital care labor, as are trans people of color more generally—trans crowdfunding is not exempt from the burdens of feminized and racialized care labor. It is not an accident that trans women and trans people of color took on a great deal of care labor in t4t crowdfunding efforts during the COVID-19 crisis, through pandemic mutual aid relief and groups such as Trans Santa and GLITS House. It is not a coincidence that multiply marginalized trans people in my local t4t mutual aid Facebook groups are the ones bumping up request posts all day long in a vain attempt to get around the algorithm that some believe purposely demotes mutual aid posts. Similarly, we must ask ourselves difficult questions about the ways that t4t crowdfunding is complicit in the stratification of deservingness. As one example, in the two medical crowdfunding campaigns I shared above, both for nonbinary people of color, only the one that was able to draw on a large social network and articulate an eloquent campaign narrative was able to reach their financial goal. While we are deeply indebted to well-known trans activists, academics, or celebrities who may have done extraordinary work in our communities, we also have to ask whether those trans people who are more famous, popular, articulate, educated, and/or attractive are more deserving of our scarce resources. This is not to make a utilitarian argument but, rather, to push us to ask tough questions about the strategies we use in the work of our collective liberation.

It is also important to consider the "bad" affects of trauma and guilt attached to the caring labor of t4t crowdfunding. Especially in transition-related medical crowdfunding campaigns, an affect of trauma circulates in which grown trans people desire to recuperate a friendlier youth or transition than we had: we redistribute funds as an investment in a future potentiality of trans life that is grounded in mourning and loss. In Trans Santa there is an affective labor of bearing witness to suffering, of trans youth becoming grievable subjects (Butler 2010), that is nonetheless anchored in a cultural obsession with trans kids. Similarly, care and solidarity are evidenced in the rapid and extraordinary crowdfunding that enabled the success of the GLITS House and the COVID-19 Mutual Aid Fund for LGBTQI+ BIPOC Folks. Nonetheless, embedded here is also an affect of white guilt that will not always yield such successful financial results as it did in the particular political moment when these campaigns circulated. This affect also circulates around the Black trans femme whose CashApp handle is shared day after day by white trans people invested in virtue signaling. This is an extractive form of care in the sense that white trans people are extracting the need to be "good" white trans subjects vis-à-vis the necropolitics of Black trans life—which does little to alter the conditions that expose Black trans femmes to precarity and premature death. White trans people may feel righteous as they pay a Black trans person via Venmo, but this is hardly a sustainable practice, given that white people's social networks are estimated to be over 90 percent white (Cox, Navarro-Rivera, and Jones 2016) and that trans people overall are much more likely to be economically marginalized than nontrans people.

If t4t crowdfunding is a durable feature of our communities, how might we harness its affect, politics, and labor of care in a way that refuses complicity in structures of domination? Employing a "revolutionary etiquette" of crowdfunding that emphasizes transparency in the purpose and uses of crowdfunding while maintaining a critique of the need for it in the first place is one such strategy (Danger and Nepon 2014; Barcelos 2020). We must also remain attentive to the tendency for crowdfunding to reproduce gendered and racial inequalities around deservingness and the uneven distribution of care labor, and work to remedy them. Recognizing what t4t crowdfunding as an affect, politics, and labor of care can and cannot do for us is a necessary related step. If t4t crowdfunding is primarily care work, we must amplify the politics of that work by tying it to political education and mobilization. There are certainly tangible affective benefits to feeling affirmed and cared for as part of a trans community (Sherman et al. 2020). But without building a shared understanding about why trans folks do not have what they need to survive and a concomitant mobilization that builds solidarity through liberation movements, t4t crowdfunding alone remains unlikely to enable us to survive and thrive. And yet, at the same time, it is an important care practice in the space between now and the revolution.

Chris Barcelos is assistant professor of women's, gender, and sexuality studies at the University of Massachusetts Boston. Their work on the politics of trans crowdfunding has been published in *Critical Public Health, Transgender Health,* and *Culture, Health, and Sexuality.*

Acknowledgements
Thank you to James McMaster for providing thoughtful feedback on an earlier draft of this article.

Notes
1.   At the time, the only exceptions were Farnel 2015 and King 2013.
2.   See Farnel 2015 as an early exception.
3.   Only 2 recipients out of 637 identified themselves as transgender in their campaign.

References

Aizura, Aren. 2017. "Communizing Care in Left Hand of Darkness." *Ada: A Journal of Gender, New Media, and Technology,* no. 12. adanewmedia.org/2017/10/issue12-aizura/.

Aizura, Aren. 2020. "The Age of the SOFFA, Trans Care, and Other Reflections on Transamory." *TSQ*Now,* December 17. www.tsqnow.online/post/the-age-of-the-soffa-trans-care-and -other-reflections-on-transamory-by-aren-aizura.

Aizura, Aren, and Hil Malatino. 2019. "We Care a Lot: Theorizing Queer and Trans Affective Labor." Syllabus for the 2019 Society for the Study of Affect Summer School.

Anderson, Mae. 2020. "Racial Equality Groups Grapple with Surge in Donations." *Chicago Sun Times,* November 25. chicago.suntimes.com/give-chicago/2020/11/25/21719692/racial -equality-groups-grapple-with-surge-in-donations-george-floyd-policing-coronavirus -giving.

Barcelos, Chris A. 2019. "'Bye-Bye Boobies': Normativity, Deservingness, and Medicalisation in Transgender Medical Crowdfunding." *Culture, Health, and Sexuality* 21, no. 12: 1394–1408.

Barcelos, Chris A. 2020. "Go Fund Inequality: The Politics of Crowdfunding Transgender Medical Care." *Critical Public Health* 30, no. 3: 330–39.

Barcelos, Chris A., and Stephanie L Budge. 2019. "Inequalities in Crowdfunding for Transgender Health Care." *Transgender Health* 4, no. 1: 81–88.

Berlant, Lauren. 2007. "Slow Death (Sovereignty, Obesity, Lateral Agency)." *Critical Inquiry* 33, no. 4: 754–80.

Berliner, Lauren S., and Nora J. Kenworthy. 2017. "Producing a Worthy Illness: Personal Crowd-funding amidst Financial Crisis." *Social Science and Medicine* 187: 233–42.

Bochicchio, Lauren, Kelsey Reeder, Lauren Aronson, Charles McTavish, and Ana Stefancic. 2021. "Understanding Factors Associated with Suicidality among Transgender and Gender-Diverse Identified Youth." *LGBT Health* 8, no. 4: 245–53.

Boston Queers for Mutual Aid. 2021. "About." Faceboook, October 10, 2021. www.facebook.com /groups/1910113582610797/about.

Butler, Judith. 2010. *Frames of War: When Is Life Grievable?* London: Verso.

Chua, Charmaine. 2020. "Abolition Is a Constant Struggle: Five Lessons from Minneapolis." *Theory and Event* 23, no. 4: S127–S147.

Cox, Daniel, Juhem Navarro-Rivera, and Robert P. Jones. 2016. *Race, Religion, and Political Affiliation of Americans' Core Social Networks.* Washington, DC: Public Religion Research Institute.

Danger, Annie, and Ezra Berkley Nepon. 2014. "Emily Post Capitalism and the Revolutionary Etiquette of Crowdfunding: A Conversation with Annie Danger by Ezra Berkley Nepon." *Grassroots Fundraising Journal,* March–April. www.anniedanger.com/wp-content/uploads /2014/03/Revolutionary_Etiquette_Crowdfunding_MarApr_2014_GFJ1.pdf.

Duffy, Brooke Erin. 2016. "The Romance of Work: Gender and Aspirational Labour in the Digital Culture Industries." *International Journal of Cultural Studies* 19, no. 4: 441–57.

Edelman, Elijah Adiv. 2020. "Beyond Resilience: Trans Coalitional Activism as Radical Self-Care." *Social Text,* no. 142: 109–30.

Farnel, Megan. 2015. "Kickstarting Trans*: The Crowdfunding of Gender/Sexual Reassignment Surgeries." *New Media and Society* 17, no. 2: 215–30.

Gill-Peterson, Jules. 2018. *Histories of the Transgender Child.* Minneapolis: University of Minnesota Press.

GoFundMe. 2020a. "COVID-19 Mutual Aid Fund for LGBTQI+ BIPOC Folks." www.gofundme .com/f/covid19-relief-fund-for-lgbtqi-bipoc folks (accessed December 29, 2020).

GoFundMe. 2020b. "Get Help with Medical Fundraising." www.gofundme.com/start/medical -fundraising (accessed December 29, 2020).

GoFundMe. 2020c "What Is Crowdfunding? The Clear and Simple Answer." www.gofundme.com /c/crowdfunding (accessed December 29, 2020).

Hilliard, David, ed. 2008. *The Black Panther Party: Service to the People.* Albuquerque: University of New Mexico Press.

Hwang, Ren-yo. 2019. "Deviant Care for Deviant Futures: QTBIPoC Radical Relationalism as Mutual Aid against Carceral Care." *TSQ* 6, no. 4: 559–78.

Jarrett, Kylie. 2014. "The Relevance of 'Women's Work': Social Reproduction and Immaterial Labor in Digital Media." *Television and New Media* 15, no. 1: 14–29.

Kenworthy, Nora J. 2019. "Crowdfunding and Global Health Disparities: An Exploratory Conceptual and Empirical Analysis." *Globalization and Health* 15, no. 1: 1–13.

Kenworthy, Nora, Zhihang Dong, Anne Montgomery, Emily Fuller, and Lauren Berliner. 2020. "A Cross-sectional Study of Social Inequities in Medical Crowdfunding Campaigns in the United States." *PLOS One* 15, no. 3: e0229760.

Kimseylove, Colleen, Todd Edwards, and David Inwards-Breland. 2020. "Effect of Medicaid Expansion on the Crowdfunding Behavior of Transgender Adolescents." *Sexuality Research and Social Policy* 18: 1–11.

King, Nia. 2013. "Will You Sponsor My Surgery? Race, Gender, and Crowdfunding." *Make/Shift,* no. 14: 29–30.

Kneese, Tamara. 2020. "Pay It Forward: Crowdfunding Is Not Mutual Aid." *Real Life,* June 22. reallifemag.com/pay-it-forward/.

Kouri-Towe, Natalie. 2020. "Solidarity at a Time of Risk: Vulnerability and the Turn to Mutual Aid." *TOPIA: Canadian Journal of Cultural Studies,* no. 41: 190–98.

Lorde, Audre. 1988. *A Burst of Light.* Ithaca, NY: Firebrand.

Machuca Rose, Malú. 2019. "Giuseppe Campuzano's Afterlife: Toward a Travesti Methodology for Critique, Care, and Radical Resistance." *TSQ* 6, no. 2: 239–53.

Malatino, Hil. 2019. "Tough Breaks: Trans Rage and the Cultivation of Resilience." *Hypatia* 34, no. 1: 121–40.

Malatino, Hil. 2020. *Trans Care*. Minneapolis: University of Minnesota Press.

Manalansan, Martin F., IV. 2008. "Queering the Chain of Care Paradigm." *Scholar and Feminist Online* 6, no. 3. sfonline.barnard.edu/immigration/print_manalansan.htm.

Marvin, Amy. 2019. "Groundwork for Transfeminist Care Ethics: Sara Ruddick, Trans Children, and Solidarity in Dependency." *Hypatia* 34, no. 1: 101–20.

McMaster, James. 2020. "Revolting Self-Care: Mark Aguhar's Virtual Separatism." *American Quarterly* 72, no. 1: 181–205.

Nelson, Alondra. 2011. *Body and Soul: The Black Panther Party and the Fight against Medical Discrimination*. Minneapolis: University of Minnesota Press.

Nowell, Cecilia. 2020. "The G.L.I.T.S House Allows Homeless LGBTQ People a Place to Thrive." *Teen Vogue*, December 2. www.teenvogue.com/story/the-glits-house-allows-homeless-lgbtq-people-a-place-to-thrive.

Ortega, Francisco, and Michael Orsini. 2020. "Governing COVID-19 without Government in Brazil: Ignorance, Neoliberal Authoritarianism, and the Collapse of Public Health Leadership." *Global Public Health* 15, no. 9: 1257–77.

Puig de la Bellacasa, María 2017. *Matters of Care: Speculative Ethics in More than Human Worlds*. Minneapolis: University of Minnesota Press.

Sherman, Athena D. F., Kristen D. Clark, Kelley Robinson, Tara Noorani, and Tonia Poteat. 2020. "Trans* Community Connection, Health, and Wellbeing: A Systematic Review." *LGBT Health* 7, no. 1: 1–14.

Spade, Dean. 2020a. *Mutual Aid: Building Solidarity during This Crisis (and the Next)*. London: Verso.

Spade, Dean. 2020b. "Solidarity Not Charity: Mutual Aid for Mobilization and Survival." *Social Text*, no. 142: 131–51.

Street, Mikelle. 2020a. "Indya Moore Is Making a Merry Christmas for Trans Youth—You Can Help." *Out*, December 11. www.out.com/activism/2020/12/11/indya-moore-christmas-trans-youth-transsanta-help.

Street, Mikelle. 2020b. "Indya Moore Raised over $20,000 for Pandemic Relief." *Out*, April 20. www.out.com/celebs/2020/4/20/indya-moore-raised-over-20000-pandemic-relief.

Tandy, Katie. 2015. "Trans Day of Remembrance Is Resilience above All." *Medium* (blog), November 20. medium.com/the-establishment/trans-day-of-remembrance-is-resilience-above-all-2e542fd6b147.

Ticktin, Miriam. 2020. "Building a Feminist Commons in the Time of COVID-19." *Signs*. Feminists Theorize COVID-19: A Symposium. signsjournal.org/covid/ticktin/.

Ward, Jane. 2010. "Gender Labor: Transmen, Femmes, and Collective Work of Transgression." *Sexualities* 13, no. 2: 236–54.

"The Transgender Craze Seducing Our [Sons]"; or, All the Trans Guys Are Just Dating Each Other

CASSIUS ADAIR and AREN AIZURA

Abstract Recent antitrans discourses have critiqued trans masculinity in particular as a site of social panic and contagion for proto-trans adolescents. In extreme cases, this is framed as a seduction. Turning "seduction" from a social danger to a benefit, this essay theorizes masc4masc t4t erotics as a type of contagious gendering. The authors discuss the coming into identity that takes place via desire for trans people, including a sexual urge toward or attraction to people who look like the person one wants to be. They examine the cultural representations of ftm4ftm erotics, and what it means to think about these relationships now, in the face of their new emergence as cultural threat. The authors make a close reading of 2000s-era erotica and pornography to argue that Daddy/boy and group sex dynamics can be read as gender labor, affective and intersubjective work that produces gender and that in t4t erotics works within a framework of differentiated reciprocity. The article concludes by gesturing toward future possibilities for trans masc 4 trans masc politics and pleasures.
Keywords transmasculinity, pornography, erotics, t4t, contagion

> But simply loving you wrenches my identity out of shape as severely as a shot of testosterone.
> —Pat Califia, "Love Sees No Gender"

> Desire can be seen as a foundation to imagine the world we want so that fantasy becomes lived, on a small scale, in daily life . . .
> —micha cárdenas, *Trans Desire*

I t's important to read Patrick Califia's "Love Sees No Gender," published in his essay/porn collection *No Mercy* in 2000, in as transfaggy a way as possible. The piece opens with Califia, who then identified as a lesbian, a "mean bitch or a leather man," fussing around his apartment.[1] He's waiting for Mike, his new trans masc

TSQ: Transgender Studies Quarterly ∗ Volume 9, Number 1 ∗ February 2022
DOI 10.1215/23289252-9475509 © 2022 Duke University Press

lover, to arrive. When he does, Mike's total assurance cuts through the nervous tension, exposing Califia as not just lusting but in love. "I can't make myself sit close to you," Califia writes, "Still, you reach me well enough, and you put your hand on my thigh. . . . The heat from your hand moves through to my jeans within a split second. I am afraid to look at you, because if I meet your eye, I might start laughing hysterically or shriek" (2000: 127). The story sets up a familiar arc: someone will get fucked, someone will come, and Califia will enumerate in careful detail every hard nipple, every slick gob of Probe lube. In this particular story, however, the plotline reveals more. As Califia narrates himself rehearsing every proto-trans move in the queer sex arsenal, from getting under the covers so Mike can't see his body, to dissociating when someone touches his cunt, to worrying that strapping on a dick makes him a misogynist, he wonders why he, a lesbian, feels "excluded" from Mike's masculinity. The lovers don't talk about the sameness they both know is there. Califia ends on a bittersweet note, anxious and awake after Mike (like a stereotypical guy) has passed out postorgasm, while Califia thinks about "pitching lit cigars into the Grand Canyon." If that's not a metaphor for transmasc dick, we don't know what is.

Although it fronts as an erotic fantasy, "Love Sees No Gender" captures all the fluttering nerves of a proto-transmasculine bildungsroman, even as Califia's authorial *I* denies this identification (this disavowal, too, another fluttering nerve). In taking this form, Califa's narrative argues that sex transmits transness. This is potentially a transgressive conclusion. As hordes of anti-trans feminists yell about the "contagion" of rapid onset gender dysphoria (ROGD), it may feel difficult to admit that in fact, yes, many of us discovered we were trans through being seduced by a trans person, just like Califia. Or, at the very least, by finding a trans person unbearably hot.

Such an admission isn't necessarily new—we are not the first or only people to discuss the plain fact of erotic intersubjectivity as a formative experience in trans life.[2] But it is still taboo. Historically, Euro-American medical discourses of transsexuality framed "gay" or "same-sex" attraction as antithetical to the ideal of producing respectable trans people who would blend in with straight society posttransition. Now, with the publication of books such as Abigail Shrier's *Irreversible Damage: The Transgender Craze Seducing Our Daughters* (2020), trans men and trans masculine people are finding ourselves framed as transmitters of a viral craze for transsexuality. As indicated by the subtitle of the book, this encodes eroticism as contagious, while claiming that trans masculinity is merely a hysterical symptom of female adolescent angst, like cutting or body image issues. These tropes recycle lesbian community myths of butch flight and the "ftm fad" that date back at least twenty years, framed as new and directed at a larger audience.[3]

Responses from within trans communities often counter that there is no "ftm fad," and that trans masculinity is neither new nor socially transmissible

(Karlan 2019). Yet this response leaves a host of questions: Why shouldn't trans-ness be transmissible or contagious? Why can't the erotic be a site of producing trans identity or practices? Why must we accommodate the asexual connotations of *transgender* when it replaces *transsexuality*, rather than asking how, as Jules Gill-Peterson writes, trans and sex work on each other (Aizura et al. 2021: 138)? Thus in this essay we interrogate a masc4masc t4t erotics, not as a site of social support or solidarity but as a site of identity formation: a type of contagious gendering through which a crush on or a desire to fuck a trans person produces a recogni-tion of the self in the other.[4]

Such an interest diverges somewhat from contemporary theories of t4t, in which questions of solidarity and sociality have loomed larger than sexuality. *T4t* began its life on Craigslist as an erotic designation, yet it has traveled far from its roots. From Hil Malatino's work, we recognize t4t as the complex web of "recog-nition, attraction, solidarity, and support" (2019: 652), a form of "antiutopian . . . solidarity" found in Torrey Peters's *Infect Your Friends and Loved Ones* (2016). As Malatino points out, the erotic dynamic between the two central trans women in this novel is simultaneously teased and foreclosed on. Yet ultimately both the novel and Malatino splinter the Craigslistian *t4t* designation from its sexual origins, defining *t4t* as a form of mutual support between trans women: a "promise to love trans girls above all else" (Peters 2016: 54). But what type of love is this, we wonder? Is it permissible that the same term that describes this trans-girl sepa-ratist praxis also describes the sweaty palms and needy cunts of Pat's proto-ftm4ftm encounter with Mike?

The ambiguity of *t4t*'s erotic meanings demands a serious consideration when applied to trans masculine relationality, and trans masculine sexuality in particular. To avoid appropriating t4t as a paradigm from trans women, we instead take seriously those instances when trans masc t4t erotic dynamics become sites of transphobic fantasy and therefore have political and material stakes. In doing so, we acknowledge that transmasc sexuality has not been widely studied because it has historically been less of a social problem for cis people, whereas trans women, in the transmisogynist imagination, are routinely hypersexualized and therefore have become the target of intensive pathologization. By contrast, many dominant cultural figures of trans masculinity over the last decade are buttoned-down/button-downed, bow-tied, and juvenile (when trans masc sexuality is figured as anything at all).[5] This aesthetic abjures erotics as at best frivolous or apolitical, or at worst, as emblematic of toxic masculinity.[6] We read this denial and disap-pearance as a symptom of how ubiquitous the (white) transmasc subject became as an erotic/aesthetic icon within North American trans/queer culture in the 2000s–2010s: think of *Original Plumbing* magazine and Buck Angel's body of porn, two examples of sexualized trans masculinity of that time, each consumed by trans subjects with rapacity yet subject to numerous intracommunity debates about the obnoxiousness of their creators.[7] The overvaluing of (white, skinny) masculinity in queer, and especially "assigned female at birth" (AFAB), erotic economies operated to exclude trans women. Perhaps this has resulted in a reluctance to revisit such an embarrassing aspect of trans cultural history.[8] However, we are compelled to look specifically at masc4masc t4t erotics in part because of the radical disjuncture between our community knowledge of ftm4ftm relationships and their abundance (and drama), versus critical analyses of such relationships, which are so scant that it seems that all the trans guy scholars must be fucking one another and thus are simply too busy to write at all.[9]

We also assert that it is worth asking what happens when trans boys or men (or bois or boiz or guys or mascs or whatever) have sex with each other. We have seen how transphobic interpretations of proto-trans masculine sexualities are increasingly part of a "feminist" rhetoric that vilifies trans masculinity for its supposedly transmissible character. Instead we argue that these projections reveal the richness of t4t erotic possiblity that undergirds trans masculine transition narratives. Finally, we think about how masc4masc t4t erotic lifeways function as an open secret in trans cultural life and argue for a way to discuss these pleasures and practices as doing important social work.

What follows, then, is a loose assembling of cultural texts—personal essays, archival snippets, fiction, pornography—read with an eye for the gendering potentiality of fucking a trans masc while you are, or are almost, a trans masc yourself. To organize these objects, we have divided this essay into three parts, which are (gayly) bound up with one other. First, we discuss the coming into identity that, we propose, actually can happen via desire for trans people, including a sexual urge toward or attraction to people who look like the person one wants to be. Second, we dig deeper into the cultural representations of ftm4ftm erotics and what it means to think about these relationships now, in the face of their new emergence as cultural threat. Third, we look at erotica and pornography to investigate how Daddy/boy and group sex dynamics can be read as gender labor, affective and intersubjective work that produces gender and that in t4t erotics works within a framework of differentiated reciprocity. We conclude by gesturing toward future possibilities for trans masc 4 trans masc politics and pleasures.

"The Transgender Craze Seducing Your [Son]" / The Trans Erotic as Social Contagion

Describing sexuality and sexual encounters as sites of identity formation shouldn't be radical or controversial to talk about. Cis people do it all the time: all erotic desires might be sites of identity formation, for anyone. But erotics and identity in trans people have been so thoroughly pathologized that even discussing it can be difficult. This pathologization has commonly been attached to trans women's sexual practices. However, an updated instantiation of this old story shifts the blame to trans mascs: the pseudo-psychiatric condition of rapid onset gender dysphoria (ROGD), which purports to account for why the people assigned female at birth are now seeking hormone replacement therapy or gender affirming treatment in larger numbers. The ROGD advocates believe adolescents are mistakenly coming to believe they are trans via being "exposed" to transness through trans and queer social media communities via what Lisa Littman (2019) calls "peer contagion." Pushed simultaneously by gender-critical "feminists" and right-wing evangelicals who believe that "gender ideology" is destroying society, ROGD uses manufactured, pseudoscientific language to spread misinformation about the evidence that transition is beneficial (Ashley 2020) and to convert anxious parents of trans teens and young adults to the misguided conviction their children are under the influence of a cult. Abigail Shrier's best seller *Irreversible Damage* (2020) narrates a popular version of the ROGD thesis: published by a conservative press, the book features interviews with parents of young trans people, purporting to show how kids are discovering trans as an internet craze. *Irreversible Damage* and others within its genre capitalize on parents' disorientation or refusal to acknowledge transness in their children, while claiming to support trans people by showing how they are vulnerable to false consciousness. In doing so, they cite "scholarship" on ROGD, which then circulates as legitimate. We cite this work with the caveat that scholars such as Florence Ashley have issued comprehensive critiques of ROGD (Ashley 2020; Restar 2020). We are not interested in relating to ROGD and gender-critical ideology as valid scientific theories; rather, we embrace the trope of contagion within them in order to investigate how trans studies can figure the erotics and identifications of young trans mascs.

Lisa Marchiano's "Outbreak: On Transgender Teens and Psychic Epidemics" (2017) provides an account of the social media/social contagion theory that is emblematic of ROGD advocates and gender-critical feminism. Marchiano is especially concerned with what she sees as "the number of teens and tweens suddenly coming out as transgender without a prior history of discomfort with their sex" (345). She finds the culprit in social media use. Marchiano's major objection is that very online trans or proto-trans teens like each other. She reserves particular pique for online media that track individuals' gender transitions and serve as a location to find community. In her view, these offer opportunities for sinister "in-group validation," as evidenced by the enthusiastic comments Marchiano quotes from one YouTuber's (uncited and unnamed) top surgery vlog:

> Can't believe how far you've come! You are amazing in every way!
> So proud and happy for you.
> You are totally rad.
> By the way, you are totally attractive.

Through their exposure to trans masc aesthetics as "cool," Marchiano claims, the commenters are apparently likely to become trans themselves.[10]

If we linger at the fourth comment, "By the way, you are totally attractive," which Marchiano leaves hanging as a type of denouement, we observe that Marchiano does not describe who finds this young "ftm" attractive, nor does she note the identities of who is cheering him on. Empirically, there is no evidence that an adolescent, aspiring trans man authored these comments. But let us assume, as Marchiano does, that at least some of the individuals watching these "transition videos" are doing so with a curiosity that is not voyeuristic but aspirational. Marchiano's citation, with its left turn from cheerleading enthusiasm to expression of sexual or romantic interest, implies that proto-trans mascs finding trans mascs "totally attractive" is dangerous. The YouTuber's alleged handsomeness quite literally figures as seductive and enticing.

But erotic desire also functions as a possible preventative of ROGD. Marchiano quotes an anonymous "Concerned Parent" on the anti-trans website Fourthwavenow, who relates how her child's trans guy therapist assures her that her child doesn't need to experience a sexual or romantic relationship before deciding he is trans. The parent expresses dismay at the thought that her child might "skip the step" of sexual relationships prior to transition: "I didn't even begin to have a clear idea of who I was, as a sexual being, until after I'd had more than one relationship. It took years for me to come to know my body's nuances and intricacies, its capacity for pleasure, how I might feel in relation to another." The assumption is that cis women "naturally" form their gender identities through having sex—that gender identity is necessarily shaped by sexual or erotic experience. Tangled up in there is also a parental anxiety that one's child might have a distinct understanding of their own body, different from the mother's body—a fear that a child can form an understanding of their gender identity that is unrecognizable to the mother.[11] This exchange frames adolescent sexual encounters as premature, preceding identity development, and yet assumes that any "normal" sexual encounters will confirm a female gender identity. The anxious mother forecloses the possibility that sexual relationships, no matter how fumbling or immature, might make the adolescent more trans, rather than less. Despite their self-proclaimed attachment to feminism, these parents and the "scholars" and public commentators who amplify their voices are ultimately anxious about the possibility of young people assigned female at birth (whether cis or trans) having any socially unmanageable sexual or romantic desires. It is not surprising to find a preoccupation with erotic attraction as both a danger sign and a site of naturalization and disciplining: this is teen sex under patriarchy and carceral feminism. But ROGD exploits the fear of one's "daughter" having a "bad" erotic object choice, regardless of orientation, to reproduce the mythical innocence and vulnerability of cis femininity.

This is to say, ROGD, along with the trans panic that has accompanied it, reproduces the standard logics of sex panics. Appeals to protect childhood, framed as innocent and vulnerable, are an evergreen tactic to stir up moral panic (Rubin 1992: 271). Yet sex panics also play out racial anxieties about the preservation of white cis- and heteronormative domestic arrangements; it is no accident that anti-trans panic has reached its apex as movements for racial justice resist the real and homicidal state violence visited on cis and trans Black, brown, and immigrant children. As we see in the wave of 2021 anti-trans bills, the figure of the vulnerable child incites the expansion of legal institutions and the carceral domain. In its call for state regulation to "save" innocent girls in particular, trans panic echoes moral panic discourses aimed at saving (white) girls from sex trafficking and reproduces similar racialized logics (Baker 2019).

Transness as the Big Bad here interrupts not only the biological essentialism of trans-exclusionary thinking but also the fantasy of romantic and erotic life as oriented toward the reproduction of the family. Importantly, that fantasy can be natalist, predicated on cis reproduction of heterosexuality, or it can be homonationalist—to entertain this possibility we must only imagine the mother above as a lesbian, whose idea of learning her body's intricacies and nuances involved realizing that she was attracted to women. Since (some) same-sex sexuality has successfully been privatized and normativized, trans youth now bear the burden of a public, visible social force of "sex" that is imagined to violate the sanctified space of the middle-class nuclear family, one of the primary institutions for reproducing property and thus reproducing racial inequity. If same-sex desire has been domesticated, transness must now represent "deviant" sex. Thus it is no accident that gender-critical "feminists" and lesbians collaborate with right-wing conservatives who are also invested in restoring a white supremacist fantasy of social and biologized reproduction; the preoccupation is with saving white middle-class children who are imagined as the ideal reproducers of the nation.[12]

Herein lies, we think, part of the power of permitting erotic desire for another trans person as a thinkable and speakable engine of trans identity formation. Any trans person knows that seduction may indeed turn your daughters into sons. As Eve Kosofsky Sedgwick (1991) pointed out three decades ago in her infamous essay "How to Bring Your Kids up Gay," anxiety around such a fact pertains only if being queer is, a priori, something to be avoided.[13] Meanwhile, unfortunately for those who panic about their offspring one day becoming, or being attracted to, trans mascs, it is both ethically permissible and very hot to be a trans masc who wants to hook up with other trans mascs. Here the panic-inducing framework of "seduction" might give way to the more agentive idea of "attraction," although as we discuss in the conclusion of this essay, there's something sexy about seduction that we don't want to sacrifice on an altar of terf-avoidant respectability. As such, having established that, alas, we're all only trans because we once watched a YouTube video of a "totally attractive" trans masc describe his seventh day on T, the second part of this essay reaches into the scholarly and historical record to sketch a more robust genealogy of masc4masc trans desire.

All the Trans Guys Are Just Dating Each Other / Leather Daddies and Their [Bonus Hole] Boys

On a hot Friday night perusing the Digital Transgender Archive, and looking for quite different objects, we stumbled across a curious essay/poem called "Transgendered Times Two: Musings of a Genderqueer SOFFA," written by Zane Barlow for a 2000 issue of the newsletter *Your SOFFA VOICE*.[14] Asserting a simultaneous need for and discomfort with "soffa" spaces, which were overwhelmingly designed for women, Barlow writes to share the experience of being a "genderqueer gay FTM in a relationship with another gay FTM." In Barlow's words, this relationship is "the queerest of the queer," a mark of pride and distinction. Yet it is also a site of struggle. Barlow writes about the gaps in this mutual recognition:

> he's [*sic*] wants to transition and I'm not sure
> he passes and I don't in public
> am I man enough for him if I don't transition?
> he's a transsexual man and I'm genderqueer

As it goes on, this text illustrates not only a multidecade persistent presence of trans erotics as a site of trans becoming but also the admission that such relationships were always far more common than generally discussed in mixed cis/trans company. "With the number of FTMs/genderqueers I know dating or partnered to other FTMs/genderqueers," Barlow writes, "I think the time has finally come to admit that although trans we don't have all the answers and we too need support as lovers, friends and allies of other transguys." Then and now, the biggest story never told among all the angst about butch flight and a transgender craze is quite simple: all the trans guys are just dating each other.

Despite this, extant scholarship on trans men as sexual beings seems tethered either to the old-saw presumption of a past lesbianism, predicated on the assumption of butchness and desire for femmes, or to the agonizing ascension of trans men into straightness.[15] Increased cultural interest in gay trans men is happening, spurred in part by the republication of Lou Sullivan's diaries by Zack

Osma and Ellis Martin. This may in turn instantiate a new academic interest in the trans man as a queer erotic figure. However, it is also true that Lou was famously interested in cis (and femmey-yet-cis-adjacent) men, not other trans mascs.[16] One notable exception in scholarship is Sonny Nordmarken and Samuel Ace's poem/essay, which frames their desire for each other as the "Mutual Affinities of Organic Beings" (2018: 157). Otherwise, t4t masc4masc cultural texts appear in personal essays, poems, or pornography, to which we will return.

From our review, we note that three of the most thorough scholarly works on t4t trans masculine sexuality are about BDSM: C. Jacob Hale's essay "Leatherdyke Boys and Their Daddies" (1997), Bobby Noble's essay "Knowing Dick" (2013), and Eliza Steinbock's (2019: 92–99) reading of *Trans Entities: The Nasty Adventures of Papí and Wil* (dir. Morty Diamond, 2007). Of these, the first two specifically center Daddy/boy play. We define *Daddy/boy* here as BDSM play that situates the top or dominant as an older, fatherly figure, and the bottom or submissive as younger and/or more impressionable. As in the Califia essay with which we began this article, Daddy/boy play offers erotic possiblities for modeling and performing masculinity. This practice has a long history in cis gay erotics: as Kadji Amin notes, Daddy in cis gay sexual culture is one of the few figures through which we can eroticize older men in a sexual culture that reifies youthfulness (2017: 27). But Daddy/boy is also ubiquitous in leatherdyke culture. It can involve age play—that is, role-playing a significant age difference, or that the boy is a child—or personal service, or both, but perhaps the one constant is that Daddy/boy involves familial nurturing and care. Indeed Califia argued in 1994 that Daddy play offers "one way to make a new, nonbiological family within the subculture of self-aware pervs" (3). As Hale writes, Daddy/boy play can enable "exploration of masculine boyhoods or periods of adolescence that were missing from our lives as we developed pubescent female bodies" (1997: 227). Hale argues that Daddy/boy also allows for trans men to explore masculine forms of dominance that are sanctioned as "too confrontational" for the public leatherdyke sex spaces that he had come up in.[17] Hale's essay repeatedly returns to the submissive role, however, with boys wearing "boyish clothes and jockey shorts," taking on a boy name and a "play age," and gaining legitimacy through having a Daddy: "Daddy gave me 'reinforcement and acceptance' for being a boy" (229).

The fluidity between markedly "male" BDSM sexual practices in gay sexual subcultures and related practices in leatherdyke/ftm sexual subcultures is not a coincidence, nor is it merely mimicry. In his 2013 essay "Knowing Dick: Penetration and the Pleasure of Feminist Porn's Trans Men," Bobby Noble argues for the relevance of cis gay erotics to trans masculine sexuality. For Noble, the "gendered sexual space of 'fag' masculinity is available to trans men as a productive trope of gendered sexual receptivity" (316). In other words, faggotry is a culturally legitimated way to get fucked in one of your holes while still being a man. Noble's analysis of the "documentary" *Enough Man* (dir. Luke Woodward, 2006) shows how Daddy/boy play in particular allows trans fags to engage in penetrative sex while articulating identities that are scripted into masculinity, "convert[ing] the traumas of being differently gendered into a sexual grammar that desires to see differently" (Noble 2013: 309). In *Enough Man*, specifically gendered sexual play and the masc language of fag, Daddy, and boy belie the now-normative trans advocacy trope that "gender and sexuality are different."[18] Instead, "sexual identifications fold over and articulate through gender," producing a set of bodily acts that signify "neither understandings of sexuality reducible to gender identities, nor the sexualities of gender identifications without reiterating either gender or sexuality according to heteronormativity" (312).

The presence in the film of a more normatively masc-appearing trans Daddy, Wendell, alongside his boy Randall, "another young pre-transition FTM who identifies not only as atypically male (his terms) but also as Wendell's sexual bottom" reveals the possibility of a sexual transaction that is not merely erotic but also identitarian and pedagogical (312). RL Goldberg (2020: 211) argues that trans men learn to be men through sexual encounter as "trans fantasies of 'efficacious pedagogy.'" In reference to trans masculine porn, Goldberg argues that trans masc porn is marked by "the explicit call to identify as students and learners. The supposition here is that we are all novices and, in the process of learning, bound to err" (219).

The mutual pedagogies that Goldberg describes are scenes of gendered education (or fantasies of such education) between cis and trans partners. Pedagogical erotic dynamics must be understood differently in the transfag Daddy/boy scenes of *Enough Man*. In the scenes that Goldberg describes, the implication is that cis men are learning about transmasculinity while trans men are, reciprocably, learning about how to emerge as fully formed faggots. By contrast, Noble's reading of t4t logics in *Enough Man* does not privilege the trans Daddy with any particular access to or knowledge of masculinity. Instead we see a type of grappling, experimenting, peer education, a sort that operationalizes and fetishizes not one man's expertise in masculinity but the pleasures of both being somewhat novice, the equivalent of the new teammate being schooled in the archetypical locker-room scene, not by the wizened coach but by the swaggering team captain.

Such a theory of peer education does not seek to purify or deny the erotic nature of identification. However, as opposed to the phobic concept of ROGD described above, in which actual children and their potential current crushes or projected future sexual desires operate as a site for adult anxiety about proper gendered development and sexual object choice, we see this t4t Daddy/boy as a space of play in which trans masculine people can re-operationalize gendering and sexualization practices—social and sexual masculinization, specifically—that may have been foreclosed on during their temporal childhoods.[19]

Couches and Other Artifacts of Gender Labor

We argue here that trans sexual practices like Daddy/boy constitute a form of gender labor, that is, affective and intersubjective work that produces gender. Kai Kohlsdorf's autobiographical story "ReSexing Trans" in the 2008 anthology *Trans Love: Radical Sex, Love, and Relationships beyond the Gender Binary* features the "extremely effeminate transmasculine" narrator writing about fucking his trans partner Joe, who is his Daddy. Fucking is central to both partners' supporting each others' trans embodiment, in particular as parts of the body are resignified between two trans people who understand and experience the same dynamic. Kohlsdorf, describing how Joe loves to get fucked in the ass, relates the careful balancing act they perform to maintain Joe's masculinity while bottoming: "We navigate his conflicted feelings of wanting to be topped and his fears of losing his masculinity by reaffirming he's Daddy even when I top him. After he cums, he usually asks for validation that I do not think he is any less of a man" (109). Again, following Noble, "sexual identifications fold over and articulate through gender," or, perhaps in this case, gender is articulated through a flexible erotic role that allows for the pleasure of bottoming.[20]

Like Zane Barlow, Kohlsdorf presents himself and Joe as both locating different configurations of transness over the course of being in a relationship. When they began dating, he writes, Joe identified as female. By contrast, Kohlsdorf himself was taking T and "struggling with the tranny hierarchy of those who . . . were taking hormones seeming to be more trans than me" (109). As Kohlsdorf relates, the two eventually "flipped about": he stopped taking T, while Joe began researching surgery and hormones. Kohlsdorf's droll metaphor for this is grounded in the power exchange of BDSM: "We had the top war and he won" (110). For Kohlsdorf and his partner, topping and dominance thus stage the need to be desired and regarded as masculine.

Indeed, Kohlsdorf explicitly identifies how sex enables a feeling of recognition and grounding that can enable a person to transition. Kohlsdorf describes how, prior to coming out as trans, Joe would not have permitted Kohlsdorf to fuck him in the ass. At that stage, early in their relationship, "his dominance was much more important to him, because that was the only tangible way he could feel male before identifying as trans" (110). As Joe begins to identify publicly as trans and receives validation as male in other parts of his life, their sexual configuration changes, and it bears less weight: "Our sex, in which he is dominant, now serves as validation where it used to serve as his only recourse to himself" (110). Thus Kohlsdorf makes the argument that the couple's t4t erotics laid the groundwork for his partner's embracing of transness: "It took our sex, and my acceptance and acknowledgment of his masculinity, for him to come out as trans" (110). While Kohlsdorf locates this enabling in the context of the intimacy and privacy of an apparently monogamous romantic BDSM partnership, the capacity of BDSM to do the work of resignifying gender identity, even to the extent that it acts as a transmission of a trans self-concept, might work in any context: monogamous, anonymous, or otherwise.

Being a good boy for your Daddy, or being a good Daddy to your boy, are here not merely pedagogy but a form of what Jane Ward (2010) names as gender labor. Ward coins the term *gender labor* to theorize the tasks of "witnessing, nurturing, validating, fulfilling, authenticating, special knowing, and secret-keeping" that she argues constitute the work of femmes who partner with trans men (240). In Ward's terms, gender is "always already bound up with the search for people and things that will offer relief, compensate for failure, enhance dignity, and create moments of realness" (240). Gender labor, therefore, is a way of meeting the trans need for such relief, compensation, dignity, and realness in the form of care work. While she acknowledges that many kinds of gendered subjects perform gender labor, Ward argues that feminine subjects are held particularly responsible for the work of gendering because the emotional tasks that comprise it are encoded as female work.[21] Sex is an important site through which this takes place: femmes who date trans men need to prove that they understand trans masculine "vocabularies of the body" (246). Sexual encounters between femmes and trans guys are not just intimate but constitute intimate labor, marked by attributes such as "trust, privacy, secret knowledge, and special access" (247). Ward concludes that femme labor reproduces trans guy identity, and that these labors maintain a crummy trans/nontrans binary and reproduce misogynist invocations for women to perform the emotional work of intimacy.

Gender labor is a useful rubric to understand how, in queer relationships that appear to have "transcended" heteronormative dynamics like the gendered division of labor, the care work of the relationship can still inequitably fall along gendered lines. Yet as an analytic to think transness specifically, gender labor falls apart precisely because, of course, cis people in relationships with cis people (c4c?) also perform gender labor. Trans people are also called on to affirm that their transness does not disrupt a cis partner's cisness or straightness. By valorizing the femme-trans guy couple form, Ward also loses a sense of how gender labor might take place outside the couple form, or in ways that are more supple, reciprocal, or communal.

Yet it's useful to continue thinking with gender labor in the context of erotic and sexual practices, and ask what happens when trans people perform it for each other in the context of t4t. What gender labor do femme trans lesbians do for each other? What gender labor might two (or three, or four, or five) trans guys do for each other? It is helpful to rethink Kohlsdorf and Joe's erotic practices within Daddy/boy as gender labors here: acts that, while not reciprocal, also do not require either partner to "silence" themselves or require an unwelcome adjustment of self or sexual horizon. For Kohlsdorf and Joe, gender labor renders transness contagious in that sex opens a path for a trans subject to intersubjectively recognize transness in another subject, a nurturing space in which that not-yet-trans subject can feel safe, and to mirror or reflect an experimental self in terms of somatic and sexual intimacy before the risk of "public" coming out becomes an issue.

Trans guy porn beyond Daddy/boy also presents moments of erotic gender labor.[22] What we noticed when looking for masc t4t porn, aside from its rareness, is that many of these films portray erotic encounters as coextensive with community or social affairs.[23] *Brunch Bunch: Queerly SF* (2010), for example, produced by TWood Pictures, features James Darling, Syd Blakovich, and seven others.[24] Opening with footage of pre-gentrification Dolores Park, the film begins with a number of trans boys walking into an apartment for a key party. The actors all look white, with the exception of one Black performer, Dale Ryder. They all inhabit trans masculinity in different ways: some have had top surgery and some haven't; some are clearly on T, some aren't. The masculine bodies in this porn do not reproduce the ripped, ultra-masc genre present in much cis gay porn but are instead slender and less hairy if at all. The performers' haircuts and dress— basketball shirts, shorts, baggy pants—deliberately frame them as youthful. This style draws on gay twink aesthetics, but even more on an aughts-era US trans masc aesthetic that eroticized looking like a cis teen boy or Justin Bieber. (We might recall Hale's point that *boy* can allow for a rewriting of adolescence as masculine here.) In the living room of a Mission apartment with bare retro fittings and bay windows, the performers sit on a large red couch or stand against the wall nervously exchanging stories about cruising—"he had little cut-off Daisy Dukes and he was getting a blowjob through his pocket"—before the film cuts to two boys in the kitchen fucking each other.

A subsequent scene brings us back to the living room, where four boys are still sitting on the red couch talking. "How do you all feel about 'boy' as a safe word?" asks Peter Piper, a specimen in a sailor cap whose self-possession and deadpan delivery of this line marks him as both predatory and a little more toppy than the others. Piper then gets shit started by undressing his friend and slapping his face.[25] Meanwhile Darling and Dale Ryder are making out in the background, visible at moments as they undress. The camera pulls back to frame both couples playing beside each other. No one in these scenes is stone, and the narrative doesn't rely on any performer signifying as older, wiser, or especially dominant. Daddy isn't home.

The couch fulfills two important functions in *Brunch Bunch*. One is cinematic, to provide the framing in order to film simultaneous scenes happening at once. The other is erotic and social, to cement the spatial conditions under which these boys are rendered into a social group or pack. Erotic intimacy takes place through sociality. And the gender labor being performed, in contrast with the earnest romance in Barlow's or Kohlsdorf's essays, reads as both playful and ironic. BDSM is a ubiquitous but unremarked part of this—the performers slap, punch, and spank each other, or face-fuck each other, but the film is not marketed as specific kink porn. This impact play rather than ejaculation or cum shots provides dramatic tension.[26]

Trannywood Gone Wild (2012), another TWood film that bills itself as a "hot transguy gay porn," also revolves around trans masc erotic sociality. In a scene that is so laid-back that it feels like an outtake, we're in the foyer of Eros as Rowan MacLachlan, Dorian Darkalley, and Dale Ryder stand around and swap jokes. The camera operator rolls tape as each fiddles with his harness and strapon. A few seconds later they're in a back room, and one of the guys is trying to wrap a towel around his erect silicon dick. The cock keeps popping out from under the towel. Cue lots of laughter: the joke is, of course, that a cis dick, with its more variable states of turgidity, might not protrude so vigorously from under standard bathhouse apparel. "It's a curse," someone says as the cock pops out from under the towel again. He finally drapes the towel over the dick, like a flag, and everyone laughs. Then they talk shop about the Spare Parts dick harness, which every person in these films appears to own. There's an ease and humor to these exchanges. Eventually MacLachlan and Darkalley move to a kind of indoor corral, where they stick their dicks through a gap in the wood palings. For what feels like a long time, the camera just captures the two silicon dicks pumping slowly, side by side, with no one in sight. The camera cuts once or twice to Dale Ryder, who is sitting nearby watching—possibly about to give them both blowjobs. But the dicks just sway in the wind. Eventually, after a too long pause, Ryder appears and starts sucking them off.

The amateurish production values of both films provide a sense that this pornography is about "just hanging out," bros experimenting with other bros. This alongside the actual sex and the dialogue—in *Queerly SF* perhaps improvised and in *Trannywood Gone Wild* clearly not scripted—produces a vacation or summer camp atmosphere. It recalls the grappling, experimenting, and peer education that Noble notes in *Enough Man*. This feels reminiscent of aughts-era trans masc culture wherein guys early on in their transitions seemed to roam in packs through activist settings, support groups, and social spaces, helping each other find binders or do T shots, constantly negotiating whether they were crushing on each other or whether they were more into women, femmes, cis gays, and so forth. Couches were essential locations in these roamings: useful for playing video games, watching movies, drinking beer, and avoiding touching each other or sitting closer and closer to each other. Sex was often an unacknowledged presence. These porn movies reproduce this aesthetic and affective space while rendering sex explicit, permissible, and mundane. While in retrospect this porn feels juvenile, bracketing as it does the whiteness of the scene and the fetishization of the bro, it also offers a way into masc t4t erotics that do not feel apologetic.

In the different cultural texts we've read here, t4t sex eroticizes the difference that can emerge in what seems like an attraction to sameness: the mutual aid vibe that flows through the "be you, fuck you." Despite how the porn we've written about here reproduces a particular aesthetic and is overwhelmingly white, it does not reproduce a transnormative body: the performers' identification with trans as a capacious opening appears far more important than bodily uniformity. In doing so, they reveal an open secret of trans masc t4t sexuality, presenting "play" that involves nurture, care, and intimacy, as jokey as it feels.

Conclusion: "A Gate We All Know We All Want"

To conclude, we envision what might result when we push trans masc t4t beyond itself, or what we've used to "represent" it in this essay. Our determination to establish a resistant masc4masc space within a t4t paradigm is indebted to a sentiment that courses hotly through the veins of trans women's literary cultures. Trans women date and fuck and teach each other in stories all the time. This can be found in the collected works of Torrey Peters (most recently in *Detransition, Baby*), as well as in Casey Plett's *Safe Girl to Love*. There are hints of t4t projection-mentorship-intimacy in the canonically awkward relationship between James and Maria in Imogen Binnie's *Nevada* (2013). We find t4t woven throughout the collaborative work of Mirha-Soleil Ross and Xanthra Phillippa MacKay, if we read their zine *Gendertrash from Hell* as love letters. In thinking with trans women's t4t culture, we are not asserting that masc4masc t4t constitutes an essentially gendered difference. Instead, we are pointing trans masculine scholarship back toward those trans cultures already spearheaded by women writers, asking what knowledge we can gain by thinking these movements together.

In her early book *Trans Desire*, micha cárdenas (2010) constructs a theory of transfeminine gender identity around the collapse between wanting to be and wanting to fuck. "How do you tell the difference," cárdenas writes, "between wanting tits, and cunt, / And wanting them in your mouth, / And wanting them against your face, / And wanting your own? / How close can I get to them" (38)? In part, this is cárdenas's glorious rebuttal to autogynephilia: a switchy *so what* of the genre that we, from a trans masc lens, also attempt above. But it is also a poetic and introspective look at the work of trans erotics for their own sake, stitching together the threads of subcultural knowledge/archival absence, pedagogical pornography, and identity formation that have propelled us through this essay. From there she investigates the critical potential of share-alike queer pornography as an explicit vehicle for "developing new somatic practices of gender and sexuality beyond male and female heterosexual coupling by documenting these practices and opening them up to propagation by sharing these photographs publicly" (51).

Repurposing the phobic association between queerness and disease, cárdenas ironically prefigures the social contagion thesis by admitting that, in fact, erotic desire for trans bodies and sexual practices can and should help spread transness. She writes, "We are trying to make these practices sexy, contagious, spreading these new practices as far as possible by creating networks of content sharing and production." Transness, through desire for trans bodies, spreads virally: "It also acts as biopolitical information vectors, spreading embodied resistant desires." In what we can only imagine is Littman and colleagues' worst nightmare, cárdenas continues to argue that, "with pornography, this function of the imagined subject in the fantasy can operate like the mirror stage, where the subject imagines themselves one way and gradually becomes that" (52). Ultimately, this self-transformation in the hot light of desire is a form, not just of trans self-fashioning but of a trans politic: "Desire can be seen as a foundation to imagine the world we want so that fantasy becomes lived, on a small scale, in daily life" (72).

So far, trans masc scholars before us have not proposed such an unabashedly sexy theory of transsexual identity formation and political life. As we argue throughout this article, we believe that now is the time to do so. We desperately need to anticipate the emergent rhetorics of anti-trans sexual panic and draw a line in the sand around our right to find each other through our crushes, our hookups, or our 24/7 Daddy/boy dynamics, and for other soon-to-be mascs or other AFAB trans people to do the same. While the cultural texts that already exist aren't yet enough, they point us toward erotic modes that we need now.

Trans mascs can draw inspiration from the tactical reversals that trans women and others who experience transmisogyny have used to reclaim their erotics (t4t and otherwise) from pathologizing and predatory frameworks, but only if we abandon the weird respectable compulsory homosociality of trans masc life. We will not be made to feel that trans masc mutual desire is some type of villainous seduction. And yet, given the toxicity of so much masculinity, it is important to assert that masculinity is not, necessarily, always violent. It follows that we should not argue that *seduction* is a phobic term, in Shrier and others, for attraction: the assertion that seduction can be a form of transformative pleasure makes space for people of many genders to enact a less panicked form of sexuality. At the same time, we mark that the stakes to reclaiming seduction are high. Seducer narratives are boring, insofar as they are clearly recognizable from panicked tropes about cisgender gay men mapped lazily on to trans queer men and mascs; they are dangerous, insofar as they presume to control and delimit the lives and loves of trans individuals.

And yet: trans seduction is beautiful. In his poem "t4t," Oliver Baez Bendorf (2020) teases us with a glimpse of this unabashed and bright-eyed trans masc for trans masc desire. In a playful resignification of the chromosomal *XX* into a hint at the pornographic sign *XXX*, Bendorf writes, "Brother. I think about his XX all the time. It's like a joke, / that we'll start dreaming of men once we." A trans masc reader, aware of the common in-community trope that trans men come out as gay after starting hormones and/or discovering Grindr, might readily supply the end of this foreshortened line as "once we transition"; Bendorf, on the other hand, refuses to provide outsiders with this subcultural knowledge. (We presume; we have no idea how cis people might read this poem, which sings so clearly to us.) A night-swimming adventure, "our clothes scattered around pine root," soon morphs into a sexual reverie: "If I had the chance," thinks the narrator, "I'd go right to the root of him." Wanting to root another trans man, after all, seems only natural, as natural as the pine: "Shouldn't I out of anyone feel it with my main medium," the speaker asks, the sonic twinship between "the root of him" and "my medium" confusing any attempt to contrast soft insides with hard protrusions. Going right in, "right to the root," is revealed to be something both deeply penetrative and surprisingly plain: Bendorf's speaker simply reflects that "there's something happy and right about us mating." In this second *right*, the right of directness merges into the right of correct, or even the right of, Oh baby, that feels so right. As the poem ends, we see, as in cárdenas, a hint of the universal seduction of this trans for trans love, an erotics so pleasurable, so "right," that it cannot remain underground. As the two come together, the "house creaks," loud enough to be heard over the wind. "Somewhere swings open a gate we all know we all want": the message of this encounter is poised to spread outside the confines of the bedroom, of the home, to go forth and teach other trans mascs that they are allowed to desire for themselves what these two have found.

Cassius Adair is a visiting assistant professor of media, culture, and communication at New York University.

Aren Aizura is associate professor of gender, women, and sexuality studies at the University of Minnesota.

Notes

1. Califia, according to Wikipedia, started hormone-replacement therapy in 1999; *No Mercy* appeared in 2000 under the name "Pat," with no pronouns in his author bio. We use male pronouns to refer to him in this essay, despite his identification at the time.
2. See Sandy Stone on the open secret of "wringing the turkey's neck," an act of presurgical masturbation subculturally discussed among trans women (1992: 159), and Eliza Steinbock's discussion of trans docu-porn (2019: 61–106).
3. A San Francisco–based newspaper published a story about whether trans masculinity was a "fad" (Rafkin 2003).

4.   We had difficulty naming "masc4masc" t4t for this essay, given the difficulty of defining *masc* and our desire not to equate masculinity with any particular configuration of iden-tification, body modification, or appearance. At times we say ftm4ftm, masc4masc t4t, and transfaggotry, but none of these are entirely adequate. We hope it is obvious, given the texts we cite, that this category for us refers to many different kinds of bodies and sexual/erotic dynamics.

5.   Scholarly citations for the claim of nerdy transmasculine desexualization are difficult to come by. Bringing these discursive formations into this essay risks scholarly impropriety, but it also usefully illustrates the extent to which meaning making on trans masc sex-ualities is still emergent.

6.   Potentially part of a subcultural backlash to the violent characterization of "Max" on *The L-Word*. See Banks 2021.

7.   Controversies surrounding Buck Angel may be found merely by attending to his Twitter account, in which he aligns himself with gender-critical feminists. For its part, *Original Plumbing* always presented a diverse range of interview subjects and models and produced little return for its editors. However, controversy sometimes surrounded *Original Plumbing*. In 2015 the TGI Justice Project called on *Original Plumbing* to reschedule a trans march after-party that conflicted with a TGI Justice Project fundraiser. See TGIJP 2015.

8.   For a critical insider representation of the erotic fetishization of skinny, white, "smooth" trans men, see the short story "An Exquisite Vulnerability" by Cyd Nova (2012).

9.   We do not mean to imply that there is no work on transmasc sexuality at all, but the majority of work on trans masc sexuality and sex work focuses on trans men's relation-ships with cis women or cis men. For more, see Pfeffer 2014; Steinbock and Davy 2012; Latham 2016; and Jones 2020. We discuss exceptions to this trend below.

10.   On trans vlogs, see Raun 2016; Horak 2014; Dame 2013; and Udy 2018.

11.   This insight is indebted to Jules Gill-Peterson's (2019) ethical insistence that the lives of trans children not be subsumed by the desires of adults, either cis or trans.

12.   For instance, while Marchiano and Shrier barely name the race and class of their interview participants, both Shrier's interviewees and Marchiano's subjects largely appear to be affluent, college educated, and white.

13.   Recognizing that this essay holds notions that we might now understand as transmiso-gynist in character, we also must note the clear parallel between the claims that Sedgwick is rejecting in 1989 and those that we are rejecting in this essay. We do so to underscore that Littman and Marchiano recycle an old cultural story about gender and sexuality, although attaching it to "tomboys" instead of "effeminate boys."

14.   SOFFA stands for "significant others, friends, family, and allies" of trans people and was used as an umbrella term to describe nontrans allies, and it often referred to sexual/ romantic partners of trans men, most often cis women. The newsletter also included a regular column, "FTM Men Loving FTM Men."

15.   For a review of the extant sociological literature on trans masc sexualities, see Rowniak and Chesla 2013.

16.   That said, while Sullivan isn't a t4t subject, in our anecdotal observations his diaries cir-culate among a very ftm4ftm readership. The publication of *We Both Laughed in Pleasure* may be looked back on as initiating not just an increased popular recognition of gay trans men in general, but also the construction of a fandom-like social network that brings t4t trans masc readers into community with one another, including (we believe) through anachronistic t4t desires for Lou himself.

17. Hale wrote in a leather subculture in which the Daddy/boy play he experienced happened mostly within leatherdyke scenes, by butch or genderqueer leatherdykes who identified as women (importantly cis and trans women are included in that category) *and* people who identified as trans men, and people someplace in between.

18. A full genealogy of the consolidation of the "gender and sexuality are different" trope is beyond the scope of this essay. For an important decolonial critique of "white produced trans 101s" and their reliance on this argument, see binaohan 2014.

19. Following Amin, we want to suspend the assumption that Daddy/boy happens only between consenting adults to insulate it from "deviance." That is to say, we think that probably, because of the way the internet works, some sixteen-year-old trans boys may be experimenting with Daddy/boy play, and that is, for the purposes of this essay, their business.

20. Thanks to Sony Coráñez Bolton, Michael Pascual, and Malcolm Tariq for their ongoing conversation with one author regarding "bottom studies."

21. In likening gender labor to emotional labor, Ward skirts the Marxist feminist debate about whether *emotional labor*, a term Arlie Hochschild (1983) coined to describe paid employees like flight attendants' labors to make consumers of service work comfortable, is useful to describe unpaid and intimate relations.

22. While a number of independent trans 4 trans masc porn films have been produced over the last twenty years, it is rare compared to the profusion of other kinds of "queer" porn. Other mainly US-produced films we do not address here include *Cubby Holes: Trans Men in Action* (TWood Pictures, 2008), a couple of FTM fucker films (dir. James Darling), and scenes made for nofauxxx.com and the Crash Pad Series. Much of this content is now unavailable because directors either stopped distributing DVDs or moved on. Recent trans guy porn is predicated on trans men fucking more mainstream gay porn performers, for example, *Bonus Hole Boys*, produced by Cyd St. Vincent.

23. *Trans Entities: The Nasty Adventures of Papí and Wil* (Diamond 2007) is a notable exception in that it features a couple, Papí Coxx and Wil, introducing their submissive Chris for one scene.

24. TWood Pictures (previously named Trannywood Pictures) produced six or seven feature-length porn films featuring and focused on trans guys. TWood DVDs arrived with educational literature, and the films explicitly model safe sex—condoms, gloves, and dental dams.

25. We assume Piper uses *he*/*him* pronouns here, although given it's a porn film, we suspect the pronouns of the character are less important than the projections of the viewer.

26. When the performers cum, they tend to cum at the same time, and viewers get to witness something we've both noticed in t4t sex, which is that sometimes a top who's fucking someone with their hand will gasp, yelp, and pant like they are also about to cum. (Our hands are our cocks: this is understood.)

References

Aizura, Aren Z., Marquis Bey, Toby Beauchamp, Treva Ellison, Jules Gill-Peterson, and Eliza Steinbock. 2021. "Thinking with Trans Now." *Social Text*, no. 145: 125–47.

Amin, Kadji. 2017. *Disturbing Attachments: Genet, Modern Pederasty, and Queer History*. Durham, NC: Duke University Press.

Ashley, Florence. 2020. "A Critical Commentary on 'Rapid-Onset Gender Dysphoria.'" *Sociological Review* 68, no. 4: 779–99. https://doi.org/10.1177/0038026120934693.

Baker, Carrie N. 2019. "Racialized Rescue Narratives in Public Discourses on Youth Prostitution and Sex Trafficking in the United States." *Politics and Gender* 15, no. 4: 773–800.

Banks, Beck. 2021. "A Visible Absence: Transmasculine People on the Screen." *Participations* 18, no. 1. www.participations.org/Volume%2018/Issue%201/4.pdf.

Barlow, Zane. 2000. "Transgendered Times Two: Musings of a Genderqueer SOFFA." *Your SOFFA VOICE* 3, no 2: 2–5.

Bendorf, Oliver Baez. 2020. "t4t." *Poetry*, January. www.poetryfoundation.org/poetrymagazine /poems/151771/t4t.

Berlant, Lauren, and Michael Warner. 1994. "Sex in Public." *Critical Inquiry* 24, no. 2: 547–57.

binaohan, b. 2014. *decolonizing trans/gender 101*. Toronto: Biyuti.

Binnie, Imogen. 2013. *Nevada*. New York: Topside.

Brunch Bunch: Queerly SF. 2010. TWood Pictures.

Califia, Patrick. 1994. *Doing It for Daddy: Short and Sexy Fiction about a Very Forbidden Fantasy*. San Francisco: Alyson.

Califia, Patrick. 2000. *No Mercy*. Los Angeles: Alyson.

cárdenas, micha. 2010. *Trans Desire*. New York: Atropos.

Dame, Avery. 2013. "'I'm Your Hero? Like Me?': The Role of 'Expert' in the Trans Male Vlog." *Journal of Language and Sexuality* 2, no. 1: 40–69.

Davy, Zowie, and Steinbock, Eliza. 2012. "'Sexing Up' Bodily Aesthetics: Notes towards Theorizing Trans Sexuality." In *Sexualities: Past Reflections and Future Directions*, edited by Sally Hines and Yvette Taylor, 266–85. New York: Palgrave Macmillan.

Diamond, Morty, dir. 2007. *Trans Entities: The Nasty Love of Papí and Wil*.

Gill-Peterson, Jules. 2019. "On Wanting Trans Women and Children (for Better or for Worse)." *Rambling*, November 26. the-rambling.com/2019/11/26/issue6-gill-peterson/.

Goldberg, RL. 2020. "Staging Pedagogy in Trans Masculine Porn." *TSQ* 7, no. 2: 208–21.

Hale, C. Jacob. 1997. "Leatherdyke Boys and Their Daddies: How to Have Sex without Women or Men." *Social Text*, nos. 52–53: 223–36.

Hochschild, Arlie. 1983. *The Managed Heart: Commercialization of Human Feeling*. Berkeley: University of California Press.

Horak, Laura. 2014. "Trans on YouTube: Intimacy, Visibility, Temporality." *TSQ* 1, no. 4: 572–85. https://doi.org/10.1215/23289252-2815255.

Jones, Angela. 2020. "Where the Trans Men and Enbies At? Cissexism, Sexual Threat, and the Study of Sex Work." *Sociological Compass* 14, no 2: 1–15.

Karlan, Sarah. 2019. "Here's What Older Trans and Nonbinary People Want You to Know." *Buzzfeed News*, January 21. www.buzzfeednews.com/article/skarlan/heres-what-older-trans-and -nonbinary-people-want-you-to-know.

Kohlsdorf, Kai. 2008. "ReSexing Trans." In *Trans Love: Radical Sex, Love, and Relationships beyond the Gender Binary*, edited by Morty Diamond, 108–111. San Francisco: Manic D Press.

Latham, J. R. 2016. "'Trans Men' Sexual Narrative-Practices: Introducing STS to Trans and Sexuality Studies." *Sexualities* 19, no 3: 347–68.

Littman, Lisa. 2019. "Parent Reports of Adolescents and Young Adults Perceived to Show Signs of a Rapid Onset of Gender Dysphoria." *PloS One* 14, no. 3: e0214157.

Malatino, Hil. 2019. "Future Fatigue: Trans Intimacies and Trans Presents (or How to Survive the Interregnum)." *TSQ* 6, no. 4: 635–58.

Marchiano, Lisa. 2017. "Outbreak: On Transgender Teens and Psychic Epidemics." *Psychological Perspectives* 60, no 3: 345–66.

Noble, Bobby. 2013. "Knowing Dick: Penetration and the Pleasure of Feminist Porn's Trans Men." In *The Feminist Porn Book*, edited by Celine Parreñas Shimizu, Constance Penley, Mireille Miller-Young, and Tristan Taormino, 303–19. New York: Feminist Press.

Nordmarken, Sonny, and Samuel Ace. 2018. "Transfiguring Desire: Divining the Origin of Species." *Journal of Lesbian Studies* 22, no. 2: 153–64.

Nova, Cyd. 2012. "An Exquisite Vulnerability." In *The Collection*, edited by Tom Leger, 195–200. New York: Topside.

Peters, Torrey. 2016. *Infect Your Friends and Loved Ones*. Self-Published.

Pfeffer, Carla A. 2014. "Making Space for Trans Sexualities." *Journal of Homosexuality* 61, no 5: 597–604.

Rafkin, Louise. 2003. "Straddling Sexes." *SFGate*, June 22. www.sfgate.com/magazine/article /Straddling-Sexes-Young-lesbians-transitioning-2607642.php.

Raun, Tobias. 2016. *Out Online: Trans Self-Representation and Community Building on YouTube*. London: Routledge.

Restar, A. J. 2020. "Methodological Critique of Littman's (2018) Parental-Respondents Accounts of 'Rapid-Onset Gender Dysphoria.'" *Archives of Sexual Behavior* 49, no. 1: 61–66. doi .org/10.1007/s10508-019-1453-2.

Rowniak, Stefan R., and Catherine A. Chesla. 2013. "Coming Out for a Third Time: Transmen, Sexual Orientation, and Identity." *Archives of Sexual Behavior*, no. 42: 449–461.

Rubin, Gayle. 1992. "Thinking Sex: Notes for a Radical Theory of the Politics of Sexuality." In *Pleasure and Danger: Exploring Female Sexuality*, edited by Carole S. Vance, 267–93. London: Pandora.

Sedgwick, Eve Kosofsky. 1991. "How to Bring Your Kids Up Gay." *Social Text*, no. 29: 18–27.

Shrier, Abigail. 2020. *Irreversible Damage: The Transgender Craze Seducing Our Daughters*. Washington, DC: Regnery.

Steinbock, Eliza. 2019. *Shimmering Images: Trans Cinema, Embodiment, and the Aesthetics of Change*. Durham, NC: Duke University Press.

Stone, Sandy. 1992. "The *Empire* Strikes Back: A Posttranssexual Manifesto." *Camera Obscura*, no. 29: 150–76.

TGIJP (TGI Justice Project). 2015. "An Open Letter to *Original Plumbing* Magazine." Facebook, June 25. www.facebook.com/TGIJP/posts/10153384813246445.

Trannywood Gone Wild. 2012. TWood Pictures.

Udy, Dan. 2018. "'Am I Gonna Become Famous When I Get My Boobs Done?': Surgery and Celebrity in *Gigi Gorgeous: This Is Everything*." *TSQ* 5, no. 2: 275–80. https://doi.org/10.1215/23289252 -4348708.

Ward, Jane. 2010. "Gender Labor: Transmen, Femmes, and Collective Work of Transgression." *Sexualities* 13, no. 2: 236–54.

Woodward, Luke, dir. 2006. *Enough Man*.

Truck Sluts, Petrosexual Countrysides, and Trashy Environmentalisms

NICHOLAS TYLER REICH

Abstract If the climate crisis, undergirded as it is by oil dependency, can be called "cis" insofar as it is driven by cisheteronormativity, then it requires a response to oil that is broadly trans—transgender, transspecies, trans-corporeal, trans-material. Rural petro-masculine iconography elides and erases our oil dependencies by pretending to a total control over fossil fuels and thereby a control over cultural and material formations of stable, binaric gender and sex. To think outside these foreclosures of both nonbinaric genders and oil's animacy, this essay introduces readers to *Truck Sluts*, an Instagram account that puts rural trucking culture at the center of a three-fold t4t exchange: trans-for-trans, trans-for-trucks, and a more expansive trans-for-trans* that crosses materialities. The author argues that *Truck Sluts* explicitly models these kinds of exchange and that doing so unseats the cisheterosexism of the petro-masculine rural, which is necessarily environmentalist work.
Keywords oil, trucks, trans-corporeal, rural, environmentalism

#transtrucksfromhell, #gonecuntry, #t4t4t4t4ever

Trans-for-Trans, Trans-for-Trucks, Trans-for-Trans*

Taking pleasure in oil is an act of violence. Gasoline is a patriarchal weapon. Sexed and gendered fossil fuels can only be toxic. Rural ignorance impedes Earth's salvation. To ruffle these entrenched ideas, my essay introduces readers to a radically rural, gender outlaw, insidiously sexy, intimately dangerous, fossil-fueled archive of photographs concisely named *Truck Sluts*. This Instagram account models t4t three ways, as trans-for-trans in the sense that a desirous exchange occurs between trans media makers and trans audiences, and also as trans-for-trucks in the sense of trans "truck fucking" and cyborgian body building. Even further, it manifests a third more expansive trans-for-trans* in the affective, trans-corporeal, desirous exchange between trans bodies, oil, and petro-machinery. In this last iteration of t4t*, I'm using *trans** to gloss identity as well as other kinds of constitutional relations and movements figured by the prefixial *trans-*. With *Truck Sluts* as case study, I articulate an iteration of what Nicole Seymour (2018) calls "trashy environmentalisms," in which ecological meaning is achieved through ironic, irreverent, low-class, and dirty means, asking: If the rural iconography of the working truck along with its petrol life fluids can be trans*ed, what new highways open between a petrol dream, rural ecology, and a trans* futurity? Although it is easy to see oil as exemplary of all that is disastrous in the Petro-Capitalocene, what trans* potential lies in oil as a technology of affective and material becoming? In other words, can trans* refigure an oil imaginary beyond disaster and into a t4t* ecological assemblage, not to save oil but to understand it more clearly?

This essay lives in the slippery confluence of trans and queer theories, energy humanities, "new" materialisms, and rural studies. I'm fascinated by the prefixial *trans-* in *trans-corporeal* (Alaimo 2010) as it relates to trans studies; what t4t* can show us about the Petro-Capitalocene's gender formations that we don't already know; and how trans*ing oil, or oiling trans*, can be an ethical way of rethinking the Anthropocene, not simply reproducing the resource fetishism that helped create all this trouble in the first place. I situate these concerns in emerging discourses on petro-cultural gender trouble, including what Stacy Alaimo (2016) has called "carbon-heavy masculinity" and what Cara Daggett (2018) has called "petro-masculinity." According to both Alaimo and Daggett, petro-fetishism and cishet hypermasculinity have reached a fevered imbroglio in late-stage capitalism. Fossil fuel overuse has become a masculine defense performance triggered against threats to both gender and climate trouble. Take, for instance, the so-called Trump Highway Rallies leading up to the 2020 presidential election (Kahn 2020). Donald Trump's populist thesis—white male nationalism and climate denialism—was embodied in massive caravans of smoke-belching, coal-rolling, exhaust-retching megatrucks with MAGA flags clapping in the wind. By controlling the oil in their engines, or so they thought, shaping it into a techno-affective experience of domination, the rally drivers also sought to control certain cultural formations of binaric gender, stable and predictable sex, resource allocation, proud extraction, and the privileged position of middle-class whiteness. What's more, this kind of petro-masculine trucking culture predominantly takes the rural as performance space. Unseating such a material and affective hegemony will require loosening from the inside, an intimate deterioration of that matter control, which in turn speaks to cultural control. Oil cannot be theirs alone, seeing what they've done with it.

With this in mind, *Trucks Sluts* models how t4t* redistributes oleaginous power in the rural, both our power over oil and oil's power over us. Transgender is fundamental to this archive's gender troubling of the petro-masculine. Its broader trans*ness, too, opens up opportunity for rethinking the materiality of fossil fuels and their gendering social powers. I turn to Mel Y. Chen's (2012) "animacy" and a trans*ed trans-corporeality to speculate about how a trans revision of rural trucking culture rebukes petro-masculinity's presumed control over all forms of matter.[1] Oil and trans taken together reshape transference across not just species but also materials organic and geological.[2] My definition of trans, in this regard, follows Susan Stryker's (2017: 1) as "the movement across a socially imposed boundary away from an unchosen starting place, rather than any particular destination or mode of transition." That unchosen starting place might refer to the Petro-Capitalocene, the petro-masculine rural, cisgender identity, the human species, or even the organic, perhaps regarded in one frightening amalgamation. Coming face-to-face with oil's animacy, its sexy and gendered sway over human species' being and the materiality of our bodies, is anti-Anthropocenic work, a shearing of andro- and anthropocentrism. If the climate crisis, or oil dependency, can be called "cis" insofar as it is driven by cisheteronormativity, then it requires a response that is broadly trans—transgender, transspecies, trans-corporeal, trans-material. *Truck Sluts* is a bumptious political site for such thinking.

I've divided the rest of this essay into three sections. In the first, I introduce readers to *Truck Sluts*, glossing its history and mechanics, discussing how these images trouble relations between sex, gender, sexuality, pornography, and rural iconography. The t4t here relies on queer strategies of camp and disidentification for its revision of the rural. This is not to say that queer and trans are easily distinguishable in the archive, but that the archive is doing many kinds of work simultaneously. Next, I discuss how petrosexual aesthetics in *Truck Sluts* productively eroticizes trans rural entanglements with fossil fuels and combustion engines. This section describes the trans* work undergirding the *Truck Sluts* brand of queered rurality. Last, I describe how this archive composes a "trashy environmentalism," harnessing the technicities of oil and trans* to translate working truck iconography into a sexy signifier with the potential for opening up more complicated ecological thought. The reader will have to excuse the smell of gasoline along the way. Or, better yet, enjoy it.

Making Trucks Gay since 1982

Petro-masculine rural trouble covers over seething material enmeshments. Uncovering those enmeshments reveals potential for thinking oil in deeper ecological terms. Likewise, doing so can help rural queer and trans people find modes of living that make better sense to them. When Donna J. Haraway (2016) compelled environmental scholars to "stay with the trouble," maybe this isn't exactly what she had in mind. But the trouble of oil and petro-masculine rurality cannot be solved by only those people who do not (critically) love or understand it. *Truck Sluts* stays with the trouble.[3]

Tiffany Saint-Bunny began this project nearly seven years ago with the Instagram account CoolTruckZone (Parker 2020). "I'm . . . a trans woman and gay. . . . It felt bad to always feel like you had to choose one or the other," she says in an interview with *Autostraddle*, "like you could be into all this shit [trucks, beer, guns] or be queer, but not both, you know, and it felt wrong to me" (Parker 2020). As CoolTruckZone attracted more followers, Saint-Bunny's project grew from a kind of personal collection of truck images (mostly framing the trucks themselves) into what is now a "pinup platform for rural and redneck queers," taking on the new moniker *Truck Sluts* (Parker 2020).[4] Saint-Bunny tells *Kerrang!*,

> You have these Punisher skull-wearing, Thin Blue Line assholes, and they see "Trucksluts" and they think, "Oh cool—trucks, sluts, this is my shit!" Then they get on there and they see it's a bunch of homos, and they're like, "What the fuck!" and get real pissed off. I think they feel like Trucksluts is tricking them or appropriating their culture or something. And that comes around to the point of, that's not their culture. That shit belongs to everyone. (Krovatin 2020)[5]

Disruption is at the center of this mediated becoming. And so is staying. And so is oil.

These days, *Truck Sluts* is still an Instagram-mediated archive. Saint-Bunny and her team source and curate photographs for the account from their more than forty thousand followers, who submit truck love from around the world. The resulting archive has a notably unified aesthetic, "sometimes sweet, sometimes seductive, and at other times an especially campy type of raunch" (Jackson 2019). The sexiness and growing popularity of these images puts *Truck Sluts* at odds with Instagram's bowdlerizing practices. "With every bump in visibility the Truck Sluts account gets," writes Jhoni Jackson (2019) for *Paper*, "the potential for shadowbanning and policing by Instagram inevitably increases," hence the occasional digital sticker covering nipples, genitals, and assholes. This censorship drives the archive toward print publication: "For now, it lives on the internet and in the hearts and groins of freak-ass homos the world over. By spring 2020, it will hit the stands as an honest to goddess porno-mag" (Saint-Bunny 2020). This history of trans mediation through erotic imaging informs *Truck Sluts* as a t4t pornography dedicated to making space by trans sexiness and for trans sexiness—against the odds, as always.

Check out this mission statement:

> Truckslutsmag exists for people that would fuck someone just because they have a hot truck. For people that get wet when they hear that perfect exhaust note or engine rumble. For people that see a babe in mechanics overalls and just can't

contain themselves. Truckslutsmag is for people that see a ladder-rack on the back of a work truck and imagine tying someone to it. It's for folks that wanna get banged on a truck, in a truck, or *by* a truck. If you think motor oil looks good on a big round ass, then Truckslutsmag is for you. If the bright green glow of fresh coolant somehow turns you on, then you're at the right place. It's like Cronenberg's "Crash," but trashier and more gay. (Saint-Bunny 2020)

I will return to trans-corporeal sex and truck fucking in the next section. For now, though, I would like to focus on how this mission statement operates within and disrupts a particularly rural aesthetic. Countrysides often register as dangerous, forsaken, and dull in metronormative formations of regionality. Jack Halberstam (2005: 27), who coined the term *metronormative*, has written on "the immensely complex relations that make rural America a site of horror and degradation in the urban imagination." The taken-for-granted social and political conservatism, racism, cisheterosexism, and generalized cultural backwardness of US (and international) ruralities put queer and trans rural art between a rock and a hard place. The queer and trans rural, in particular, struggles against the sexually violent and cisheterosexist narratives seared into rural American visual history in the likes of *Deliverance* on the one hand and *Boys Don't Cry* on the other. I'm reminded of trans memoirist Eli Clare's ([1999] 2015: 42) "feeling queer in the queer community" as a backwoods outsider. The results of these pressures, in both popular rural art and criticism, tend toward visibility politics, metronormative assimilation, and apologist aesthetics.

    Truck Sluts makes no such concessions. This archive simultaneously respects, fetishizes, and lampoons prototypical rural aesthetics. But at no point does this mixed-up approach invite queer and trans city slickers to laugh at the rural petro-masculine, rather than with or alongside its revision. In other words, the elaborate disidentification at work here does not rely on a metronormative apology. *Trucks Sluts* reimagines rural trucking from within as a disidentification emerging from both frustration and understanding. In this regard, what we can notice right away through this archive is an ethic of salvage. These aren't the "souped-up" megaton trucks of the petro-masculine ideal, which is largely a gentrification of rural trucking that seeks to ironically bedazzle working-class reliance through chromatica, expensive lift kits, woof-ed up sound systems, and countless other enhancements, both cosmetic and (dys)functional. These aesthetics speak to Daggett's point that petro-masculinity embroils American wealth, energy exceptionalism, and militarism as wards against economic anxiety, a veneer that pretends toward working-class utility but is really anything but (29). Instead, *Truck Sluts* vehicles are the mostly practical, used, workhorse, and "living" trucks of a presumably low-income contributing collective. Moreover, as with any

Figure 1. Blue and Vidisha tease BDSM aesthetics on the back of a carpentry truck (*Truck Sluts Magazine* 2020).

disidentification, *Truck Sluts* is not finished with its reference culture. It does not intend to leave behind or forsake its unchosen petro-masculine starting place. Rather, *Truck Sluts* intends to stay, and salvage, to better understand rural trouble.

Figure 1 captures rurality in a strange light. Blue, bracing on the tailgate of this working truck, presses their boot down onto Vidisha's face. With their chains and leather (or maybe pleather, a petroleum product), these two limn the iconographic space between working-class rurality and urban trans club scene, both potentially and serendipitously signified in the icon of the hammer. The deep indigo of Vidisha's ensemble tethers with the hammer, a likewise blue headlight shining on this scene where queer and trans people *are* the rednecks, performing within that iconograph's relational field. The truck bed cache of busted rocks, accumulated from a day's work, imbues the diegesis with the heft of labor. Vidisha's goat-horn strap, upcycled from a roadkill, is both a threat to the pelvis and a fetishizing of the road's many dangers. They hold it at the ready.

What does it mean to "sweat together towards a new universe," as the caption of this image reads? A "new universe" could be one where the spaces between public and private, work and sex are not so sanctioned, a gap cleaving rural conservatism and metronormativity. Figure 1's trashed-up, salvaged pornography reorients the working truck as a site for bucking the kinds of surveillance and regulation many queer and trans people experience as particularly strong in rural spaces, from both petro-masculine and metronormative censors. Blue and Vidisha's BDSM instantiates what trans labor scholar Anne Balay (2017: 100)

#ilovemytruckandmytrucklovesme

#t4t	#bigtrucksnofucks	#ACAB
#unknownpleasures	#1800sludgenation	#blacklivesmatter
#makingtrucksgay	#dirtydirty	#giveyourmoneytoxworkers
#t4t4t4t4ever	#apocalypseWOW	#generalstrike
#truckslutsinternational	#keepontruckin	#shitshovelhustle
#scrapyardqueers	#WeSeeUs	#cuntrylife
#worldisafuck	#cosplayasyourowntruck	#misstrucknuts
#queerfutures	#gearfemme	#twotruckshavingsex
#enemyofthestate	#dieseldyke	#femme4femme
#censored	#southerncumfert	#butch4butch
#makingrustgay	#rustedbutnotforgotten	#oldtrucksneverdie
#builtfordbuff	#offgrid	#pussyfingersforjesus
#truckfuckersincorporated	#fuckthecistem	#assclappalachia
#homosintheholler	#horny4cornbread	#transtrucksfromhell
#artist4artist	#lifeisahighway	#buttchug4christ

#whathappensinthewoodsstaysinthewoods

Figure 2. The *Truck Sluts* tropology.

calls "sex as a form of retaliation." The new universe runs parallel to the theater of the petro-masculine, and that very proximity could be the petro-masculine's undoing, a prying away of its foothold on rural aesthetics. Blue and Vidisha simultaneously disidentify with not just cisheteronormative petro-masculine rurality and working-class order but also metronormative queerness, transnormativity, and environmentalist sanctimony, all on the back of a gas guzzler.

This process is codified into searchable language through phrases like #hornedstrapsummer and #makingtrucksgay. Hashtags function in *Truck Sluts* as a parsing of the disidentifications imagined visually in the archive. It's a kind of tropo-wayfinding through rurality as it exists in other (cishet) terms and a disidentifying with that cartographic enmeshment. I've gathered a partial collection of the *Truck Sluts* tropological imaginarium (see fig. 2). The language is parodic in the sense that few Instagram users will be searching for terms like #1800sludgenation, #fuckthecistem, or #assclappalachia. Then again, this metadata now exists in the broader Instagram compendium. A portal to the new universe opens, inscribed in a dirty new/old love language.[6]

Using both visual and tropological disidentifications, this new universe might further be one where the stratigraphies of racialized gender collapse in on themselves under the increasing, fossil-fueled pressure of their own rhetorical and visual grammars. Petro-masculine countrysides are white and cis-male. This nightmarish ideal is as false as it is pervasive, empowered over and again by the post-2016 invigoration of rural exclusionary politics, voter restriction campaigns, All Lives Matter counterprotests, anti-trans legislation across rural America, neo-Confederate Jim Crow nostalgias, and conservative panic in the face of high-profile gender and climate trouble. *Truck Sluts* works to disprove this fiction by simply making visible white queer and trans lives as well as queer and trans lives

Figure 3. @jerkdusoleil poses on hay bales (or "gay bales") in a truck bed (*Truck Sluts Magazine* 2019c).

of color being lived in rural spaces, especially in highly contested rural spaces like Appalachia and the Deep South (#homosintheholler, #hornyforcornbread, #southerncumfert). Perhaps more significantly, *Truck Sluts* revises the language and aesthetics of the "traditional" working-class rural to erode those exclusionary politics at their insidious foundation, while preserving the fabric of rural belonging as something worth holding onto for those who can't/won't afford (financially, culturally, spiritually) a migration to the queer and trans urban strongholds. Black trans in the rural is, in this way, already overdetermined by a politics of staying across the Plantationocene and its diasporas. Expressing rural trucking culture differently, and with greater attention to oil's animacy, could function as a kind of reparative fugitivity (even while staying where the captivity trouble is supposedly louder and more visible). This maneuver potentially unblocks a legacy of fungibility between Black bodies and fossil fuels—through a machine that might otherwise be used for the chase, not the escape.[7] The missing "backstory" in figure 3, for example, is glossed by its revision of Grant Wood's *American Gothic*. @jerkdusoleil, with legs provocatively spread across the pitchfork and top-surgery scars drinking in the sun where their overall strap has fallen tantalizingly aside (#overallbabe), has placed themself between the anachronism of American agricultural frontierism and its exaggerated legacy in contemporary petro-masculine rurality, neither of which foregrounds Black bodies as either the agents of nationalist hegemony or component to its homogeny. @jerkdusoleil stays right there with the trouble.

José Esteban Muñoz's original fascination with disidentification emerged from crossings over gender, race, sexuality, and materiality in often surprising and counterintuitive ways—ways that are indeed more complex than either the assimilationist or anti-assimilationist images they partially resist/revise/revisit.[8] In *A Billion Black Anthropocenes or None*, Kathyrn Yusoff (2019) speaks to material fungibility as foundational to Anthropocenic trouble, a mixing of both the substances and identities of Black(ened) people and the resources they have been forced to both extract and absorb in the toxic fallout. That original extractionist, racial capitalist, racially gendered fungibility between Black bodies and fuel can be reimagined through a trans-corporeal intimacy with oil in an affective transformation of rural space and its white petro-masculine iconographies. Through cultural and material disidentification, fungible fugitivity takes back oil and rurality from the greedy hands of the petro-masculine. Perhaps, in this instance, environmental justice looks like a Black trans redneck firing on all cylinders, making fungibility with fossil fuels fugitive in a Black Anthropocene.

Burnin' Gas and Eatin' Ass

Oil wants. We want oil. We want *with* oil. The prefixial state of trans is a prepositional orientation—becoming with, of, across, over, in, and through.[9] It's not a stretch to say that crude oil and its derivatives (re)made the human earlier in the Petro-Capitalocene. But it is necessary to think anew about how oil remakes the human ongoingly and remakes itself through the human. Attending to this transference becomes a matter of matter's desire and our desire for matter, and how that exchange reframes presumably nonliving material as capable of "casting a trans light back on the human" (Chen 2012: 128). This section looks at how other-than-human materials have the animate power to make, unmake, and remake human-animals and themselves in processes that heretofore have been overvalued and overdetermined as already gendered in specific registers (petro-masculine), rather than as processes that are enmeshed with gender emergence and world building (t4t*). I'm thinking, too, about how this exchange is engorged through the truck as machine and rural iconograph, leaning into trans strategies of allowing the body to become as it emerges with other materials, multibodied and transcorporeal. It's pivotal that the t^* in this t4t* exchange is situated around trans/gender, because both climate and gender trouble are at stake in petro-masculine world eating, which cannot be underestimated in its power to generate particular apocalypses for the excluded in favor of white cis-male supremacy.

Most energy scholars are prepared and even giddy to admit that human entanglements with oil have crossed into a maddeningly dense network of (inter)dependencies. As fuel scholar Heidi C. M. Scott (2018: 178) puts it, "We can't even see oil because we look through oil glasses . . . we are, ourselves, petroleum products, cyborgs." Oil has worked itself into our bodies through food, water, cosmetics, vapors, medicines, ability-enhancing technologies, and, even more insidiously, desires and ideas. It powers our mobility and momentum. It gives our machines strength when our bodies have none. It vibrates our flesh energetically until the source of arousal becomes indistinguishable as either outside or in. Yet its constitutivity with our emergent sex, gender, and sexuality goes unnamed. Scholars of the "geo-social," like Yusoff, have shown how fossil fuels exact control over human interactions, how they shape our sociality around extraction and fuel use, thereby expressing their own potential to desire. And scholars of the "petrosexual" have revealed connections between petro-politics, petro-violence, and misogyny by focusing on violence against women's bodies as a practice foundational to petro-masculine motives of extraction and matter control.[10] But if I change the valence of *petrosexual*, moving these gendered petro-relations firmly into the erotic, I can also move closer to what Scott (2018: 183) calls the "orgiastic power in oil's repertoire." If, as she puts it, the "epistemic inability or unwillingness to name our energy ontologies" in the twenty-first century has developed into what seems an unshakable habitus, how, then, does the orgasm shiver through (13)? And what can that orgasm tell us about the mutually constitutive relations between energy, oil, and our sexed and gendered bodies?

Truck Sluts gets at this inflected petrosexual by instantiating and fore-grounding oil's otherwise invisible libidinal, gendering energies. Figure 4 concretizes an elusive feeling of #ilovemytruckandmytrucklovesme. Here, a trans person fucks the trailer hitch of her truck with a strap. From her perspective, both the strap and the truck might function as appendagic extensions of gender and pleasure, as well as tools for bodily becoming. From another perspective, the truck, strap, and the human might all be extensions of oil's desires from the start, rather than oil acting as incidental lubricant. Pleasure is the nexus of oil's, the truck's, and the trans person's becoming, underpinning all of those possibilities routed back to oil's technical versatility and combustibility.[11] This is what Seymour (2015) has called a "trans-corporeally affective" relationship, a wild synergy of utmost acrossness parodying the boundaries built up between machine, human-animal, and oil. The revision is, again, of the petro-masculine desire, perilously suppressed, to fuck oil (and all matter) into submission. Admitting to the pleasures of trans-material fucking relaxes this suppressive pressure on oil's animacy and constitutivity such that genderings emerge that are not toxic, despite the carbon toxicities, because they are not predetermined. Transness, in other words, is shown to thrive in this materiality, which is antithetical to petro-masculine cultural astringency. Whereas petrocultures typically go hand in hand with the insistence on stable, binary genders, here we have the opposite.

In his *Countersexual Manifesto*, Paul B. Preciado (2018) describes a pros-thetic trans-material ontology in which the dildo precedes the dick, or artifice

truckslutsmag • Following

truckslutsmag Do you love your truck as much as my tiz @woodsqueer loves hers? Come see this and many other new works at my solo show this Halloween, in Cisco! Swipe for a new flyer!

And before any y'all go off half-cocked and report this, it's a plastic dick and it's Halloween week, so get a fucking grip, take a big ass breath, and move on.

#crashbycronenberg #truckfuckersinternational #t4t #strapdown #ilovemytruckandmytrucklovesme #truckslutsmagazine #makingtrucksgay #truckslutsmag

3,053 likes

OCTOBER 28, 2019

Figure 4. @woodsqueer penetrates a truck with her strap (*Truck Sluts Magazine* 2019a).

precedes the natural in a history of sexuality. "Dildonics," in his terms, is a way of rupturing the biological determinism underpinning a cis-heterocentric regime by leaning into technosexuality, or the fabrication of trans sex through prosthetic means. *Truck Sluts* might likewise seem at first glance like a movement away from "nature," fusing together the sexual becoming of queer and trans people with machines, dildos, and other material technologies—a process several *Truck Sluts* photos humorously extend to the truck itself by revising the petro-masculine stereotype of hanging steel balls from the trailer hitch, this time as an image of gender emergence, rather than determinism.[12] However, it's important to acknowledge that trucks and even dildos are petroleum products.[13] Oil undergirds all these technosexual devices—the dildo, the steel balls, the truck, and even the human body. Oil animates the kind of trans sexual fabrication Preciado describes, powerfully pointing trans back at the human as a way of being that is consistently fabricated over and again by oil's own desirous technicity.[14] This, in turn, diminishes the petro-masculine conceptualization of either truck or human gender as predetermined, rather than a process of ongoing trans-corporeal, co-constitutive becoming. *Truck Sluts* reveals that the technosexual is, in fact, not a removal of the body from nature but instead a traversal through oil-as-nature. If oil makes up the total climate in which we live, as so many energy scholars rightfully claim, acknowledging it as underpinning the technosexual would provide a more thorough theorization of the human body within a trans-corporeal environment, as well as gender writ large. *Truck Sluts* performs this back-to-nature move as a trans-for-trans* exchange.

Figure 5. @mxboombastic straddles the engine of a truck while vaping (*Truck Sluts Magazine* 2019b).

Figure 5 is an even clearer rendering of this trans-corporeally affective synergy. @mxboombastic straddles the engine of a 2007 Toyota 4Runner in a petrol-slick fuck session between human and machine. Recall the *Truck Sluts* mission statement from above. Like David Cronenberg's 1996 technosexual fetish film *Crash*, *Truck Sluts* curates a cyborgian sexiness between human and machine, powered by oil, actively gyrating on propriety. While @mxboombastic is only vaping here (#vapemastergeneral), the framing creates the illusion that their body is siphoning fumes from the truck engine, like a human flue, pulling smoke up through the genitals and dispersing it out through the mouth. Their exhalation graphs oil passing in many forms through machine, human, and environment. Alaimo (2010: 2) writes, "Imagining human corporeality as trans-corporeality, in which the human is always intermeshed with the more-than-human world, underlines the extent to which the substance of the human is ultimately inseparable from 'the environment.'" This goes not just for clean materials but also the toxic. @mxboombastic's fumes rise to meet the clouds, and a clear line forms between oil and climate with the body as ozonic transition point. Liberal environmentalist and sexual-moral sensibilities will make this a difficult image to take in for some. In the phrase "shootin guns, jumpin trucks, blowin clouds," clouds figure not only as meteorology or pollution; "blowin clouds" is also a rural euphemism for smoking methamphetamine, typically used in relation to having sex. Its evocation here puts further forms of toxicity in proximity to sexual and gender becoming.

Staying with these troubles, toxic as they are, is surely more effective than pretending they have no constitutive meaning. To be sure, as evidenced by this euphemistic cunning, not all viewers are meant to fully understand. The important point is that petro-masculine iconography has been allowed to tell only one story about oil, trucks, and pollution for too long. An invitation to a greater petro plentitude is here: #cumandtakeit.

Expanding the petro narrative, however, will not be easy. As Scott (2018: 13) points out, the collective Global North and Western human habitus around oil tends toward either an "unwillingness to name our energy ontologies" or else a doomsday modality. There's barely room for an in-between. Yet, as petro-cultural scholar Stephanie LeMenager (2014: 4) claims, with the right analytical perspective, scholars might reveal an "unprecedented devotion, even love" for oil that runs "ultradeep." *Truck Sluts* complicates oily ontologies by revealing the sexualizing and gendering potential already residing in that relational habitus. This is the technicity of oil as a material capable of generating "ultradeep" entanglements, as well as the technicity of trans as an embodied translation of that process. The iconography of the working truck and all it touches is being wholly reimagined as a movement across matter and ontology. The ultradeep surfaces.

This Environmentalism Is Trash: #fordfemtheplanet, #apocalypseWOW

Peak oil, pollution, and conservationist rhetorics make the petrosexual a dangerous aesthetic. How easy it would be to brush *Truck Sluts* under a queer anti-future analytic of the Lee Edelman variety, like some propane torch burning at the end of time or a Mad Max–ian guzzoline eschatology. But there's much more to this archive than learning to love the bomb. To reiterate: if climate change is predicated in large part on a white-nationalist petro-masculinity, its mitigation could be imagined only by an approach that takes the mutual constitutivity of gender, sex, and oil seriously. My goal here is not to bring *Truck Sluts* into the popular environmentalist fold. Moralizing environmentalists don't like this kind of fun, anyway. Instead, through *Truck Sluts*, I'm trying to understand what a different environmentalism could look like if it took this enmeshment seriously, particularly as situated around queer and trans rural living.

Beyond the plentiful theses on oil cultures as evil wholesale, some critiques seem to have already disavowed the specific kind of petro-relationality I've been exploring. Alaimo (2010: 16) writes, in a book otherwise provocatively focused on the intimate trans-material relations other environmentalists overlook: "Huge McMansions, giant trucks, and gas-guzzling SUVs (all of which contribute to the vast amounts of carbon being emitted into the atmosphere) serve to insulate their inhabitants from the world . . . fantasies of transcendence or imperviousness." This swipe at "fantasies" forecloses a desirous trans-corporeality between gas-guzzler, the gasoline guzzled, and the machinist themself—not to mention the claim toward individual responsibility for planetary salvation. There is also LeMenager's (2014: 7) affective read on the ultradeep: "We are loathe to disentangle ourselves or our definition of life from [oil]." And this "destructive attachment" constitutes what she calls a "bad love," one that impairs a healthy sense of life and environment (12). These are bad feelings with bad consequences. Leaving them to die in the ultradeep becomes a moral and ethical imperative. But LeMenager's implication that we are even capable of disentangling ourselves from oil elides our co-constitutivity with oil. There is, in this sense, a fantasy of inseparability (to play off Alaimo's term) here in LeMenager's claim.[15]

Raising these ultradeep feelings from their murky depths can help answer Seymour's (2018: 22) pivotal question: "What makes an artwork environmentalist?" Cultural works like *Truck Sluts* that wriggle around in dissident affects trouble a centralized, metronormative, and, frankly, cisheteronormative ecocritical and environmentalist approach. *Truck Sluts* features no explicit environmentalist rhetoric or functional sustainability message. Mainstream environmentalists would almost certainly dismiss this archive as environmentally ambivalent at best or anti-environmentalist at worst. Seymour's "bad environmentalism," on the other hand, makes space for the dissident and disfunctional. A bad environmentalism is an environmentalism performed wrongly—unsanctimoniously, as it happens. It poses peculiar questions that do not always lead to easy-to-equip answers. Above, I've shown how *Truck Sluts* certainly lacks any serious moral-environmentalist claims. The archive sits with a camped-up irreverence toward pollution, propriety, and petro-masculinity—inappropriately foregrounding "how matter that is considered insensate, immobile, deathly, or otherwise 'wrong' animates cultural life in important ways" (Chen 2012: 2).

Truck Sluts is, more importantly, a "trashy environmentalism" in that it surfaces the erotic feelings of the ultradeep through a pointedly class-critical t4t* exchange, toxic all the way down. Trashy environmentalisms are countermodels to a middle-class taste-making performance of environmentalism (Seymour 2018: 199). Let me say in clearest terms: mainstream environmentalists don't understand, nor do they care to understand, how fossil fuels can be so intimately intertwined with (rural) life as to become erotic. Trash, in this sense, is often taken to index a yearning for a better life—which, from a mainstream environmentalist perspective, could never necessitate an erotics of gasoline. That is dirty and wrong. Rurality, oil, and transness taken together, however, craft a revision of the petro-masculine that is not melancholic for modernity, in the condescending environmentalist sense. LeMenager (2017: 472) defines what she calls "petro-melancholia" as "an unresolvable grieving of modernity itself, as it begins to fail." This is the complex feeling of "losing something not quite anticipated," an oily future of riches and tech, as well as a past spent earning it (478). She goes as far as to say that "the inclusion of US southerners," for instance, "within the South as a *global* region has become clear" (474). This likening sees a specifically American form of rurality, a romanticized class-conscious partner to empire's industrial metro-symbolic, as a global wash with regions that have also spurned or been denied petro-progress to its furiously gleaming ends. Imperial petro-capitalism hasn't "paid off" for the rural. Yet the *Truck Sluts* archive demonstrates that petro-melancholia does not saturate its t4t* project. This archive is instead about dis-empowering rural American petro-masculine control over its own iconography, even and perhaps especially when those icons manifest American-like in other geopolitical regions. That figure 1 comes from New Delhi may surprise some readers.[16] *Truck Sluts* resists both queer cultural imperialisms and oily affective imperialisms. The queerness and transness imaged are wholly incompatible with metronormative tastes, as they don't effectively spread a message of Western queer assimilation or visibility proper. And the desires for oil and machine do not constitute a form of petro-masculine melancholia, as the desire is not for progress or power over others, whether economic or cultural. Pleasure and belonging in this archive elide LeMenager's claim that "feeling at home in a petrol 'world' creates an affective drag on thinking through human survival" (112).

Staying with the trouble is not melancholic. It is a kind of survival and homemaking practice. Muñoz (1999: 12) writes, "As a practice, disidentification does not dispel . . . contradictory elements; rather, like a melancholic subject holding on to a lost object, a disidentifying subject works to hold on to this object and invest it with new life." He would later dispel this melancholic simile alto-gether for a radical futurity. But, even here, staying is antithetical to stagnation. It's an investment in the already here. This is a counternarrative running against the "slow death and abandonment" written onto ruralities (Clare [1999] 2015: 65). Finding a way of staying is reparative. *Truck Sluts* holds the history of the ico-nography of the working truck, with all its contingent racism, misogyny, and anti-queerness/-transness, just as it pulls that imagery into another story, one that has been held hostage in the rural for some time.

There have to be ways of thinking oil outside wholesale foreclosure, if oil is indeed home. Exposing ourselves to oil's claims on our lives (Alaimo 2016), its constitutivity at nearly every level of our various ontologies, including sex and gender, seems like a terribly important strategy for beginning to understand and therefore mitigate our reliance on its powers. As oil drips through their quivering bodies, the queer and trans media makers contributing to the *Truck Sluts* archive are showing a way. Their way is t4t*, not just trans* as identity but as practice and outlook. They help us see how energy ontologies actually develop and, more spe-cifically, how rural energy ontologies are much more important than the festering mistakes they are so often thought to be.

Nicholas Tyler Reich (he/they) is a doctoral student at Vanderbilt University's Department of English, where he studies queer and trans ecologies, literatures of the US Deep South and Appalachia, and energy ontologies. Their work has been published or is forthcoming in *ISLE: Interdisciplinary Studies in Literature and Environment*, the upcoming reference book *The Encyclopedia of LGBTQIA+ Portrayals in American Film*, the upcoming edited collection *The Anthropocene: Approaches and Contexts for Literature and the Humanities*, and elsewhere.

Acknowledgments
I'd like to acknowledge and thank Nicole Seymour for graciously reading over this essay. Her feedback is premium-grade, high-octane fuel.

Notes

1. I'm thinking here of Chen's (2012: 225) read on the 2010 Macondo Prospect oil spill in the Gulf of Mexico. Chen claims that the news media's coverage of the well as "dead" (as in, no longer spilling out extraction-released toxins) linguistically sublimated the "pure animation of the oil" as a gendered tactic to mitigate anxieties around toxicity, or "hysteria."

2. Dana Luciano and Chen (2015: 184) have poetically imagined the potential in "an in/organic identification" between queer and trans bodies and material forms such as stone. They wonder whether "lifting that prohibition" of desire between the in/organic "multiplies not only the possibilities for intrahuman connection but also our ability to imagine other kinds of trans/material attachments" (185).

3. We might think about how this language of staying resonates with movements like The STAY Project (n.d.) in Central Appalachia. Though, moving for personal safety should never be confused with abandoning the rural. Staying with the trouble can be ideological and aesthetic work, if not always a physical practice of exposure to toxicities (material, ideological, petro-masculine, etc.).

4. In some instances, this archive is called *Truck Sluts Magazine*. The Instagram site name, for instance, is truckslutsmag. I've shortened to *Truck Sluts* throughout to reduce confusion.

5. Saint-Bunny is referring here to other Instagram accounts that use #trucksluts. For example, there is @trucksluts (not to be confused with @truckslutsmag), which curates images training an explicitly cishet, white male gaze on heavily modified or souped-up trucks and mostly white women with small body types posing pinup style.

6. In *A Dirty South Manifesto*, L. H. Stallings (2020: 70) argues that "sexually decolonized land politics" will be pivotal for undermining the moral semantics, and semiotics, of the so-called New South. Dirtying up, as in exposing and engorging, the latent desires in the rhetorical and iconographic staples of petro-masculine rurality weakens its exclusivity from underneath, wearing away at its project of cultural conservancy.

7. I'm thinking here of C. Riley Snorton's (2017: 55–97) invocations of Hortense Spillers and Snorton's own thinking on "fungible fugitivity," or a reworking of gender fungibility toward fugitivity. What would it look like for Black trans bodies in the rural to lean into material fungibility with fossil fuels as an inversion of histories of enslaved and incarcerated extractive labor, as well as racialized gender politics, in predominantly rural

spaces? This would inflect the use of *matter* in Snorton's observation that "there is no absolute distinction between black lives' mattering and trans lives' mattering within the rubrics of racialized gender" (x).

8. Muñoz (1999: 18) writes, "If the terms *identification* and *counteridentification* are replaced with their rough corollaries *assimilation* and *anti-assimilation*, a position such as dis-identification is open to the charge that it is merely an apolitical sidestepping, trying to avoid the trap of assimilating or adhering to different separatist or nationalist ideologies." This, as Muñoz argues, is not the case with disidentification, since its strategies are housed primarily in anti-assimilation while still resisting the normativizing practices of anti-assimilationist work (e.g., metronormativity). Disidentification is the "queer-er" position (#trufreex).

9. Eva Hayward's (2008) "becoming *with* starfish" resists the division between metaphoric and material relations; it's a metaphor that reshapes material intimacy between two ostensibly untethered life-forms, taking on a trans-corporeal significance. My treatment of oil is likewise metaphoric and material. Trans is like oil, but it is also with oil, and the two remake one another's material being.

10. Heather M. Turcotte (2011), who coined *petro-sexual*, and Sheena Wilson (2017: 273) use this term to describe how "histories of feminism and oil are intertwined," particularly in terms of petro-violence against women.

11. Balay (2018: 8) has shown how queer and trans people who drive semi-tractor-trailer trucks often conceive of the truck as both supplemental to their own strength of independence—"sharing [the truck's] power," which is to say sharing in oil's power— and a protective barrier against the threats of a marked queer or trans life on the road.

12. Cishet people, mostly men, do this to telegraph their stable masculinity, but in queer and trans hands it demonstrates that such accessories are appendagic tools, expressing a Butlerian idea that supposedly natural, stable genders (ironically) need prosthetics to achieve their appearance as natural and stable.

13. Not all but many sex toys, like those fabricated with silicon, are made from materials derived from fossil fuels, as are many lubricants—which deeply reiterates Scott's point that we *are* petroleum products.

14. I'm thinking here of Jules Gill-Peterson's (2014: 406) model of "trans as an expression of the originary technicity of the body." By relinquishing, as in acknowledging, animacy to other-than-human materials, like oil or the testosterone molecule, trans emerges along-side the material's "technical capacity for differentiation as living matter" (408).

15. I'm bringing up Alaimo and LeMenager in this way because their arguments are so important to my thinking. They trouble desire, oil, and animacy. And yet here we see that even the most provocative claims about oil remain tinged with normative thinking. I don't bring up the many cishet white men scholars who reify rural and petro demonization, because that would be too cumbersome and obvious.

16. At several United Nations climate change conferences, India has repeatedly said that it needs fossil fuels to become a more "developed" nation—and that Global North nation-states are getting to have it both ways—gobbling up fossil fuels to develop themselves, then turning against fossil fuels. Development, in this way, and as it relates to figure 1, resonates with the kind of constitutivity I've covered in this essay at the level of national sovereignty. It's a matter of unseating the petro-masculine imperial control over extracted matter, which is a global problem (Daggett 2018: 29). Rural American petro-masculine iconography is a fitting language for disidentification precisely because of its gendered and nationalist overdeterminism.

References

Alaimo, Stacy. 2010. *Bodily Natures: Science, Environment, and the Material Self*. Bloomington: Indiana University Press.

Alaimo, Stacy. 2016. *Exposed: Environmental Politics and Pleasures in Posthuman Times*. Minneapolis: University of Minnesota Press.

Balay, Anne. 2017. "Sex and Surveillance on the Highway." *TSQ* 4, no. 1: 96–111.

Balay, Anne. 2018. *Semi Queer: Inside the World of Gay, Trans, and Black Truck Drivers*. Chapel Hill: University of North Carolina Press.

Chen, Mel Y. 2012. *Animacies: Biopolitics, Racial Mattering, and Queer Affect*. Durham, NC: Duke University Press.

Clare, Eli. (1999) 2015. *Exile and Pride: Disability, Queerness, and Liberation*. Durham, NC: Duke University Press.

Daggett, Cara. 2018. "Petro-Masculinity: Fossil Fuels and Authoritarian Desire." *Millennium: Journal of International Studies* 47, no. 1: 25–44.

Gill-Peterson, Jules. 2014. "The Technical Capacities of the Body: Assembling Race, Technology, and Transgender." *TSQ* 1, no. 3: 402–18.

Halberstam, Jack. 2005. *In a Queer Time and Place: Transgender Bodies, Subcultural Lives*. New York: New York University Press.

Haraway, Donna J. 2016. *Staying with the Trouble: Making Kin in the Chthulucene*. Durham, NC: Duke University Press.

Hayward, Eva. 2008. "More Lessons from a Starfish: Prefixial Flesh and Transspeciated Selves." *WSQ* 36, nos. 3–4: 64–85.

Jackson, Jhoni. 2019. "The Rural Queers Reclaiming Redneck Culture." *Paper*, December 11. www.papermag.com/truck-sluts-instagram-interview-2641572481.html.

Kahn, Brian. 2020. "The 'Petro-Masculinity' of This Weekend's Trump Highway Rallies." *Gizmodo*, November 2. earther.gizmodo.com/the-petro-masculinity-of-this-weekends-trump-highway-ra-1845550339.

Krovatin, Chris. 2020. "Meet the Queer, Body-Positive Trucker Zine Taking Outlaw Culture Back." *Kerrang!*, March 6. www.kerrang.com/features/meet-the-queer-body-positive-trucker-taking-outlaw-culture-back/.

LeMenager, Stephanie. 2014. *Living Oil: Petroleum Culture in the American Century*. London: Oxford University Press.

LeMenager, Stephanie. 2017. "Petro-Melancholia: The BP Blowout and the Arts of Grief." In *Energy Humanities: An Anthology*, edited by Imre Szeman and Dominic Boyer, 470–85. Baltimore: Johns Hopkins University Press.

Luciano, Dana, and Mel Y. Chen. 2015. "Has the Queer Ever Been Human?" *GLQ* 21, nos. 2–3: 182–207.

Muñoz, José Esteban. 1999. *Disidentifications: Queers of Color and the Performance of Politics*. Minneapolis: University of Minnesota Press.

Parker, Lauren. 2020. "TruckSlutsMag Is Making Trucks Gay and Reclaiming Rural Queer Culture." *Autostraddle*, January 11. www.autostraddle.com/truckslutsmag-is-making-trucks-gay-and-reclaiming-rural-queer-culture/.

Preciado, Paul B. 2018. *Countersexual Manifesto*. Translated by Kevin Gerry Dunn. New York: Columbia University Press.

Saint-Bunny, Tiffany. 2020. "The Story." *Truck Sluts Magazine*, June 13. www.truckslutsmag.com/about.

Scott, Heidi C. M. 2018. *Fuel: An Ecocritical History*. London: Bloomsbury.

Seymour, Nicole. 2015. "Alligator Earrings and the Fishhook in the Face: Tragicomedy, Trans-corporeality, and Animal Drag." *TSQ* 2, no. 2: 216–79.

Seymour, Nicole. 2018. *Bad Environmentalism: Irony and Irreverence in the Ecological Age*. Minneapolis: University of Minnesota Press.

Snorton, C. Riley. 2017. *Black on Both Sides: A Racial History of Trans Identity*. Minneapolis: University of Minnesota Press.

Stallings, L. H. 2020. *A Dirty South Manifesto: Sexual Resistance and Imagination in the New South*. Oakland: University of California Press.

The STAY Project. n.d. www.thestayproject.net/what-is-stay.html (accessed May 1, 2021).

Stryker, Susan. 2017. *Transgender History: The Roots of Today's Revolution*. New York: Seal.

Truck Sluts Magazine (@truckslutsmag). 2019a. "Do you love your truck as much as my tiz @woodsqueer loves hers?" Instagram, October 28. www.instagram.com/p/B4KyGGTF8q_hCJilHE9LQAtxxe9XDCznfTCc5oo/.

Truck Sluts Magazine (@truckslutsmag). 2019b. "Got a submission cummin at y'all from @plantdaddyrandy . . . " Instagram, September 24. www.instagram.com/p/B2zMoPUlI1u-Ggl_ucF3TxcfZRIvEoV5uJSqUoo/.

Truck Sluts Magazine (@truckslutsmag). 2019c. "@jerkdusoleil sent these in without comment so I don't have a backstory, but god damn how can one person be SO HOT??" Instagram, July 4. www.instagram.com/p/BzgKB3Ul-q1oV79R_cNxfZICcxgRk6Mv2u9iBoo/.

Truck Sluts Magazine (@truckslutsmag). 2020. "We love the glow from streetlights . . . " Instagram, May 27. www.instagram.com/p/CAs5mT_DYEarN67Nok3dITEk12WSVz33yfYImMo/.

Turcotte, Heather M. 2011. "Contextualizing Petro-Sexual Politics." *Alternatives: Global, Local, Political* 36, no. 3: 200–220.

Wilson, Sheena. 2017. "Gendering Oil: Tracing Western Petrosexual Relations." In *Energy Humanities: An Anthology*, edited by Imre Szeman and Dominic Boyer, 269–84. Baltimore: Johns Hopkins University Press.

Yusoff, Kathryn. 2019. *A Billion Black Anthropocenes or None*. Minneapolis: University of Minnesota Press.

"Necessary Bonding"

On Black Trans Studies, Kinship, and Black Feminist Genealogies

AMIRA LUNDY-HARRIS

Abstract This article uses a t4t framework rooted in Black feminist thought to meditate on the convergence of Black and trans in meetings between fields, encounters with text, and relational bonds forged between individuals that help promote collective creation. Section 1 explores the bridging of Black feminist thought and trans studies in relationship to the emergence of Black trans studies. The second section examines how the searching Black trans reader's encounter with the text allows for the imagination and creation of an actualized trans self. Section 3 takes a more conventional approach to the concept of t4t, exploring the kin bonds created between Black trans people, with an eye to the way that Black feminist literature is used to describe these relationships. **Keywords** collective creation, kinship, t4t, Black feminist thought, Black trans studies

This project emerged out of my own desire for a sense of Black trans kinship—for a whole family tree, really. Years ago, when I began my transition, I dove into memoirs, the archives, and YouTube channels in search of a sense of history and some sense of a way forward. Reading and watching, I felt, tied me to those who had come before and to those who were traveling the road alongside me. This article is shaped by those encounters, which I offer in the text as a continuation of the practice of sharing of the self that has been so central to Black trans life. In doing so, it is my belief that this project itself acts as a form of kin building—the process of my writing and your reading bonding us through the text.

In this article, I argue that a Black feminist approach to t4t might not only name encounters between trans people but, more broadly, help illustrate the connections between Black and trans that describe fields, texts, and individuals. This project meditates on transness/ Blackness in the context of movement. I argue that the "trans" taken up by Black trans studies, or trans studies from a Black feminist perspective, is characterized less by transition from point A to point B and more by its study of fugitive (or insurgent, following Spillers) movement outside normativity's boundaries. This definition is built on movement's and marronage's relationships to freedom in the narratives of William and Ellen Craft and others (Craft and Craft [1860] 1999; Roberts 2015), the movement of tranifestation (Green and Ellison 2014), the concept of Sankofa, the routes of Black/queer/diaspora (Allen 2012), Black trans studies' movement of return to Black feminist thought, and the memory of water's movement and the *trans*-Atlantic slave trade (Sharpe 2016; Tinsley 2008, 2012). In this way, I borrow from Dora Silva Santana's theorization of transatlantic water, which itself builds on the work of M. Jacqui Alexander, to illustrate the fluid, expansive nature of transness. Transitioning, Silva Santana (2017: 183) suggests, "is our movement along that space of possibilities that produces embodied knowledge. It is moving across and along the waters, the imposed limits of gender." Our insurgent movement on the outside normativity's boundaries is that which moves us along the waters, closer to the horizon (Muñoz 2009: 1), the space of possibility.

This characterization of trans as fugitive movement structures the way that I approach the concept of t4t in this article. While t4t has conventionally signaled encounters between people under the trans umbrella, I argue that an approach to this framework guided by Black feminist thought opens up the opportunity to more expansively describe various forms of connection trans folks engage. This perspective on transness enables us to use the t4t framework to highlight coalitions with those perceived to be outside the boundaries of gender normativity, connections with ancestors and trancestors, and even relationships with/to narratives that help us examine our understanding of self. This expansive approach, guided by Black feminist thought, shapes the way that I utilize t4t connections in this project. In this essay, I argue that t4t might be used to think about the convergence of Black and trans in meetings between fields, encounters with text, and relational bonds forged between individuals that help promote collective creation.

In the first section, I explore how the bridging of Black feminist thought and trans studies—both fields operating at the borders of normativity—has helped foster the creation of Black trans studies. In the second section, I write about how the searching Black trans reader's encounter with the text allows for the imagination and creation of an actualized trans self. In the third section, I write more conventionally about the concept of t4t—exploring the kinship bonds created between Black trans people, with an eye to the way that Black feminist thought is used to describe and inform these relationships.

While the third section offers the most literal discussion of kinship bonds, I suggest that we might think of each of these levels of t4t encounters as a form of relational connection. Indeed, I use the language of kinship throughout this article to draw attention to the ways that the connections I explore foster collective construction. On each of these levels—the meeting of two fields that help create another field, the book that helps create a trans person, the relationship two trans people share that allows them to actualize their full selves—I ask, might this also be a form of kinship, of birthing something new? In the sections that follow, I take up this approach to t4t to explore the connections between Blackness and transness in fields, texts, and individuals.

Section 1—"White Is What Woman Is"

In this first section, I highlight the way that the emergence of Black trans studies represents a t4t connection between Black feminist thought and trans studies.[1] I use a Black feminist approach to t4t to suggest that the field of Black trans studies is a product of collective creation, not simply self-making.

Recent scholarship, characterized by *TSQ*'s "Issue of Blackness," suggests that movement toward a Black trans*/studies might in fact be a movement of return—to the foundational work of Black feminism. This move to center Black feminist thought, through citational practice and by illuminating "repressed genealogies" (Ellison et al. 2017: 164), matters because it underscores the fact that Black trans studies didn't birth itself. This acknowledgment, that Black trans studies emerges not only from trans studies but also from Black feminist thought, helps put into focus the relationship between the fields of Black feminist thought and trans studies. That space of overlap, the bridge between these two ostensibly disparate fields, offers fertile space for Black trans studies to grow. Indeed, illuminating, rather than repressing Black feminist genealogies may well help expand the field of trans studies.

As the editors of "The Issue of Blackness," Treva Ellison, Kai M. Green, Matt Richardson, and C. Riley Snorton (2017) suggest, centering Black feminist scholarship on the mutability of gender offers a generative opportunity for those of us in trans studies to reassess the boundaries of transness. In "We Got Issues" they assert, "Black/womanist/Africana feminist thought provides 'grammars' for articulating gender that exceed the rubrics of biology/biocentrism or social artifice. Careful attention to the debates in the field opens up ways for reading transness as always and already theorized and theorizable from the literature on 'racialized gender'" (165). As Ellison and colleagues highlight, careful attention to Black feminist scholarship illustrates the work that has already been done on racialized gender construction, work that isn't often characterized as foundational to the field of trans studies. Reclaiming this genealogy and centering Black feminist thought provides the opportunity to think more expansively about gender, the movement of transness.

Despite the lack of citation, Black feminist scholarship has long offered important theorization on the racialized nature of gender categorization. The thinking of Hortense J. Spillers has been particularly generative in providing grammars for Black trans studies. Spillers's theorization of ungendered Black female flesh in her groundbreaking 1987 article "Mama's Baby, Papa's Maybe: An American Grammar Book" elucidates just how central the system of chattel slavery was to the construction of gender in the United States. Spillers's analysis of enslaved Black women's experiences of various forms of sexual violence as well as the brutalities of bondage perceived to have been reserved for men provides a historical perspective on the mutable nature of Black gender (68). This description of ungendering clarifies the cost of Black women's violent exclusion from the "cult of true womanhood," a process that, as Evelynn Hammonds (1997: 173) describes, "seemed to lock black women forever outside the ideology of womanhood." What Spillers and Hammonds illustrate here—the construction of (white) womanhood on the back of Blackness—offers a point of reflection on the precarious nature of cisgender identity and its implications for the boundaries of transness. The genealogy of Black feminist scholarship on racialized gender that I highlight here provides critical interventions and foundational language for Black trans studies.

"Mama's Baby" is useful for Black trans studies, not only for its prescient description of the racialized history of gender but also for its vision of the future. Spillers's (1987) argument that, moving forward, Black people might use this history of exclusion from normative gender roles to chart a new course, offers fertile ground from which Black trans studies might theorize. Her turn away from an aspiration for normative gender toward making "a place for this different social subject" (80) lays the foundation for theorizing transness/Blackness as movement at the boundaries of normativity. Spillers envisions a way forward that is "less interested in joining the ranks of gendered femaleness than gaining the insurgent ground as female social subject" (80). As Ellison and colleagues (2017: 165) suggest, Spillers offers a way of thinking gender beyond biocentrism, a grammar that is rooted in the racial history of gender construction. This is why a return to Black feminist thought has such significant implications for trans studies, offering language and opportunities to envision transness differently. Sustained study of literature on racialized gender by scholars like Spillers highlights the opportunity for convergence of Black feminist thought and trans studies. This relationship between Black feminist thought and trans studies that comes through the study of racialized gender has been the space through which Black trans studies has emerged, thinking transness and Blackness in connection with one another. We're only beginning to see the way that an approach to investigating the connections between Black feminist thought and trans studies can shape the field of Black trans studies.

"The Issue of Blackness" presages this emergence of/in Black trans studies, using Black feminist grammars to index the ways that racialized gender exceeds the boundaries of normativity. This study of Blackness and transness in relationship to one another, or as "nodes of one another" (Bey 2017: 278), is only just starting to emerge. The very beginnings of the Black trans*/studies toward which the special issue editors theorize can be seen in texts like Kai M. Green and Marquis Bey's 2017 "Where Black Feminist Thought and Trans* Feminism Meet: A Conversation," Snorton's 2017 *Black on Both Sides: A Racial History of Trans Identity*, V Varun Chaudhry's 2019 "Trans/Coalitional Love-Politics: Black Feminisms and the Radical Possibilities of Transgender Studies," and Joshua Aiken, Jessica Marion Modi, and Olivia R. Polk's 2020 "Issued by Way of 'The Issue of Blackness.'"

Black on Both Sides offers a particularly salient meditation on the utility of centering Black feminist thought in trans studies, as Snorton (2017: 11–12) returns to "Mama's Baby" thirty years later. Spillers's influence on Snorton's project is palpable, explicitly framing the first third of the book and haunting the last two-thirds. Snorton utilizes the concept of ungendered Black female flesh to elucidate the ways that racialized gender in the United States was produced in the context of chattel slavery and its implications across time by taking up moments when Blackness exceeds the limits of so-called normative gender. By taking up the concept of fungibility, Snorton highlights a point that the field of trans studies has so often forgotten—that transgender's consolidation into identity categorization is a racial narrative.

If we consider the racial politics that constituted the creation of the term *transgender*, who—or what—does *trans* represent? And, if Black people have been locked "forever outside" normative gender categories, what radical coalitional possibilities are obstructed by organizing via identity (Cohen 1997)? These are the kinds of questions that begin to arise at the contested and generative point where Black feminist thought and trans studies connect. *Black on Both Sides* illustrates the possibilities that present themselves when we theorize transness more expansively using Black feminist grammars on racialized gender as a framework. Snorton's thinking embodies some of the critical work that is beginning to emerge from Black trans studies' investigation of the relationship between Black feminist thought and trans studies.

This innovative work centering a genealogy of Black feminist thought offers the opportunity to approach trans studies differently or from a different perspective. In this way, acknowledging this repressed genealogy of Black feminist thought not only illuminates the connection to Black trans studies, for whom it has provided language, but also illuminates the connection to trans studies as a whole—for whom it helps question the boundaries of transness. The texts that I've highlighted in this section illustrate the foundational impact of literature on racialized gender to trans studies and offer a sense of where the field might go.

Alongside this emergent group of Black trans studies scholars, I seek to expand on the work that is being done to theorize the connections between Black feminist thought and trans studies. There is still much work that can be done in Black trans studies to flesh out this relationship, and I hope that my theorization of a Black feminist approach to t4t helps in this effort. I hope to offer an intervention in the field by suggesting that a Black feminist approach to t4t might allow us to see this movement of work, exploring the relationship between Black feminist thought and trans studies, as part of a larger structure of thinking Blackness and transness in relationship to one another—on the level of fields, as well as on the level of texts and individuals.

Section 1.5—Got to Be Real

In the two sections that follow, I take up Janet Mock and her writing as case study. Here I highlight some of the reasons Mock and her work are particularly well positioned to illustrate how so often dominant descriptions of transness are stripped of any racial narrative. In a reclamation of repressed genealogies, I read Mock's work to recenter the Black feminist thought that she describes as central to her work.

In 2014, writer, director, and producer Janet Mock published her first memoir, *Redefining Realness: My Path to Womanhood, Identity, Love, and So Much More* (2014c). *Redefining Realness*, which became a *New York Times* best seller, examines themes of self-making, love, family, identity, and growth. The story explores her experiences from growing up as a trans girl of color in Hawai'i and California into the formations of her adult life in New York City. Since the book's publication, Mock has been on the *Advocate*'s 40 Under 40, the *OUT*100, the *Root* 100, and *Time*'s 100 Most Influential People lists, and she became the first out trans woman of color to be hired as a TV series writer when she began working on *Pose*. With this increase in recognition, Mock has been asked to enter highly visible mainstream spaces, in order to educate viewers on trans identity. A couple of these interviews—with Piers Morgan on CNN in 2014 and on "The Breakfast Club" in 2017—involved violently transphobic rhetoric and attacks (Mock 2014b, 2017). In this way, we can see how Mock has served—for better and for worse—as a public face of transness in the mainstream.

In her 1988 article "The Race for Theory," Barbara Christian argues that people of color have always used narrative forms to theorize, highlighting the work of Toni Morrison and Alice Walker as examples of Black women writers speculating "about the nature of life through pithy language that unmasked the power relations of their world" (68). Following Christian, I suggest that Mock's work is part of this genealogy of Black feminist writing. In a 2014 interview, Mock writes that her heroes are "women writers. I grew up with Zora Neale Hurston,

Maya Angelou, Alice Walker, Toni Morrison; they showed me so much through their work" (Kolker 2014). This is abundantly clear in her writing, highlighted in the sections that follow, and in her larger body of work, including public conversations with bell hooks on the Black female body (The New School 2014b) and with Melissa V. Harris-Perry (2014).

Despite the ways that Mock and other prominent faces of the "transgender tipping point" (The New School 2014a) have emphasized the significance of Black feminism to their work and sense of self, the narrative of the category of transgender has so often been evacuated of any racial grounding. In this way, narratives around Mock and Laverne Cox's emergence as hypervisible faces of transness have untethered them from the work of Black feminist thought. Ellison and colleagues (2017: 162) illustrate how this phenomenon plays out in trans studies, where although the "popular representation of fabulousness and the crises of the trans subject are represented primarily by Black transwomen and transwomen of color, the field of transgender studies, like other fields, seems to use this Black subject as a springboard to move toward other things, presumably white things." Instead of moving toward other, presumably white, things, this article engages in a movement of return to Black feminist thought. In this way, my decision to use *Redefining Realness* is part of my aim to recenter a racial narrative into the category of transgender, highlighting the relationship between Blackness and transness. An exploration of Mock's work from this perspective allows both a clearer reading of the work's discussion of kinship, as well as a better vision of the way that the work is part of a larger Black feminist genealogy.

Section 2—The Searching Black Trans Reader

In this section, I take a Black feminist approach to t4t to consider the relationship between the Black trans reader and the text. In doing so, I explore the ways that this encounter with the text helps produce the actualized trans self. Central to this project is the concept of collective creation, the collaborative project that is the making of the self. This concept is generative in that it names the fact that we are helped made by people we may never meet but who still help move us toward the trans self we know ourselves to be. SJ Langer (2014: 66) uses "collective construction" to describe the way that trans people benefit from those who medically transitioned before them. This thinking helps illustrate an aspect of the collective construction that I speak to in this section. That is, by others having been trans before us and by passing that information—knowledge that's cultivated from personal experience—along to us, we are able to also move closer to ourselves. What does it mean for us to create connections with one another through these texts, for us to be able to see and make ourselves through that process?

The concept of the encounter, which Avery Dame (2017: 152) describes as "that moment when a person recognizes their experience in the trans other," offers language to help answer that question. The encounter may occur while watching a television show, as Muñoz highlights in *Disidentifications* (1999: 154); by meeting someone new; or by coming across a news article, as Sandy Stone explains as part of the "obligatory transsexual file" in "The *Empire* Strikes Back" (1992: 155). Through others, we are able to gain a sense of our transness and thus a better perception of ourselves. Trans studies scholars such as Dame have highlighted the significance of the encounter to the construction and maintenance of one's sense of self as trans. The concept of the encounter—the recognition that helps you realize that you are akin to someone else out there—centers the narrative of collective creation, as opposed to self-making.

We might use this framework of the encounter in the trans literary context to theorize the relationship between the reader and the text, and imagine the process of reading as a form of kinship building. Alexander Eastwood's (2014) essay "How, Then, Might the Transsexual Read? Notes toward a Trans Literary History" helps us explore trans reading practices and the affective relationship the Black trans reader has to narrative. On building kinship through reading what has been written before, Eastwood writes, "Reading for resonance rather than for recognition allows one to develop alliances with ontologically different characters and to encounter oneself unexpectedly in the past. Resonant reading enables strange kinships between readers and texts, kinships that act as salves for the searching trans reader" (602). This searching trans reader may or may not find an explicitly trans text, but they are still able to come to know themselves better, coming closer to being the fullest version of themselves, because that text offered them a relational connection from which a deeper sense of self emerged. Eastwood's theorization of reading for resonance rather than for recognition mirrors the Black feminist framework I highlight above. Both enable us to expand our categorization of trans, to highlight the possibility of connection in the fugitive movement outside normativity's boundaries. This work helps frame a number of questions this article seeks to address: What's possible when we expand kinship's definition to more than just relationships between blood ties, or even between two humans? What might it look like for a reader to build a kinship with the text? Is it possible to care for those who come after us simply by writing down our truths? Dame, Langer, and Eastwood provide language to help answer these questions by clarifying how the literary encounter serves as a process of kinship building.

In what follows, I explore two instances of searching Black trans readers experiencing encounter across difference that enables them to see themselves more clearly. I take on the relationship—the textual kinship—between the text and the Black trans reader to explore the collective construction that emerges from this connection. This section uses Eastwood's framework of resonant reading to highlight the significance of building textual kinships with ontologically different characters. Here I illustrate how the Black trans reader's encounter with the text plays a role in the process of self-making or, more precisely, collective creation.

In a YouTube clip posted as part of the promotional rollout for *Redefining Realness*, Mock reflects on the centrality of reading in her process of finding her sense of self as a young girl. Looking back on the time she spent at the Kalihi-Palama Public Library in Hawai'i, Mock (2014a) recalls "taking *Waiting to Exhale* and like, reading it secretly because I knew it was an adult book that I wasn't supposed to read yet. I just remember words and stories. And seeing women that reflected me and looked like my image of self was so empowering." Mock's experience in this quote illustrates Eastwood's concept of the searching trans reader. Mock mentions *Waiting to Exhale*, Terry McMillan's 1992 *New York Times* best-selling romance novel exploring the love lives of four Black—ostensibly cisgender—women friends. Despite the lack of overt trans content, Mock's resonant reading enables her to forge connections across ontological difference. She describes the sense of empowerment she feels in searching for and encountering herself, her image of self, in the text. Through this process, a kinship forms between Mock, the reader, and *Waiting to Exhale*, the text.

In the YouTube clip, Mock (2014a: 0:01–1:51) goes on to describe how the instrumental role that reading played in her own self-making shaped her perspective on writing her own book as an adult:

> To think that my book will be in libraries for another young girl to see and to read and to sneak into her room—that's not a realization that I can even wrap my mind around yet. It is still so surreal, but I know that as a writer and as a storyteller and as a reader, that's a dream becoming true. That's me becoming my dream just as Janie could become the woman that she is, just as I could become the woman that I am. All of it is very much wrapped into itself and it all starts with words. Telling your truth is about your choice, your agency over being able to tell your life story. And I think that I've always yearned for that. I've always yearned for that sense of being able to create the book that I should have been able to read growing up, to be able to create and contribute to that story about the experience of growing up as a young trans girl, as a young trans girl of color. What does that look like?

On one level, Mock is thinking through the relationship—the kinship—that she has to the text as a trans writer. Mock has become the woman that she is because of her ability to create an image of self from "seeing women that reflected" her, such as Janie from *Their Eyes Were Watching God*. But part of her self-making is tied into writing this book because it is her dream turning into reality. In this way, Mock's desire for the agency to tell her truth on her own terms elucidates what has made memoir such a compelling form for trans people. On another level, Mock is thinking through the relationship the text has to the trans reader. As she imagines the reader, the young trans girl of color, taking her book home from the library and reading it, Mock asks, "What does that look like?" It looks like the moment of encounter.

My own reading of *Redefining Realness* was that moment of encounter when I recognized my experience in the text. Just as Mock formed her image of self through reading books about women that reflected her, the same was true for me. I devoured *Redefining Realness*; it was only after finishing it that I realized how long I'd been searching for texts that helped me imagine myself otherwise. Though both of us were reading across difference (cis and trans womanhood in Mock's reading of *Waiting to Exhale* and masc and femme trans identity in my reading of *Redefining Realness*), our reading for resonance as opposed to recognition still enabled a bond to form between us and the texts we read. This is precisely what I mean when I suggest that reading can be a kind of kin building, through the process of seeing yourself in the text and realizing you are akin to someone else out there. This returns us to Eastwood's (2014) concept of the trans reader and the text as salve. In writing the book that she should have had the opportunity to read when she was growing up, Mock enables the Black trans reader—in this case, me—to enter a kinship with the text, which "act[s] as salve for the searching trans reader" (602).

In the YouTube clip, Mock mentions how, in writing *Redefining Realness*, she became the woman she had always dreamed herself to be. She draws parallels between her process and the development of Janie Crawford, the protagonist in Zora Neale Hurston's seminal 1937 novel *Their Eyes Were Watching God*. Mock's creation of an image of self was strongly influenced by reading Black feminist literature such as *Their Eyes Were Watching God*. Hurston's novel has become a canonical text in Black feminist thought, after the field's own reclamation of repressed genealogies (Walker 1975), and Janie's character has remained a critical mirror for Black women readers' self-creation in the eighty years since its publication. In *Their Eyes Were Watching God*, Janie searches for love that allows her fullness; after navigating several relationships that seek to stifle her, in the end, she is able to become the woman that she is in her fullness. The journey that Janie undertakes over the course of the novel, Harris-Perry (2011: 28) suggests, is "about carving out a life that suits her authentic desires rather than conforming to the limiting, often soul-crushing expectations that others have for her. In this way, her personal journey is a model of the struggle many black women face." Resonant reading highlights the ways that Mock's experience is akin to Janie's. Following Eastwood's analysis of Ellison's *Invisible Man* (1952), we might read *Their Eyes Were Watching God* as a Black trans text, whose protagonist chooses to live a life authentic to herself instead of succumbing to the pressures that her family, partners, and society place on her.

In this section, I have sought to explore the encounter the searching Black trans reader has with the text. I have utilized a Black feminist approach to t4t to theorize the way that this relationship enables the fruition of the actualized trans self.

Section 3 — Strange Kinships

In this section, I explore the connection between Black feminism and Black trans becoming. I use t4t in a more traditional sense here, describing the kinship bonds built between trans people. Still, I center Black feminist thought in my analysis, as it shapes the way that these bonds are described. I offer a reading of a passage of the text that takes up the author's portrayal of kinship and illuminates the significance of collective creation. In this particular section of *Redefining Realness*, Mock (2014c) begins to paint a picture of the large kinship network she became a part of as a young girl in Hawai'i. She describes the community this way:

> This underground railroad of resources guided me during the years of uncertainty, giving me an agency that empowered me to take my life, my body, and my being into my own hands. Wendi and I were low-income trans girls of color. We didn't have many resources, but what we were blessed with was being at the right place at the right time. Hawaii's community of trans women was vast and knowledgeable. There was a deep legacy of trans womanhood passed on to us by older women who had been exactly where we were. And this provided us with stability despite what some view as a dramatic shift in our adolescence. (135–36)

What Mock describes in this quote is an intergenerational community—vast and knowledgeable—that ran on the sharing of knowledge and resources. Intergenerational (i.e., parent-child) connections are at the very center of the traditional nuclear family model. For those who forge kinship bonds in other ways, connections across age are not as guaranteed, certainly less built-in. For example, because many queer and trans communities are built around club/bar scenes, these networks are inaccessible for those under the legal drinking age. This segmenting of queer life by age can make it difficult for young folks to find those who have knowledge because they have "been exactly where we were." Given this context, Mock's introduction into the intergenerational underground railroad is all the more significant. While these kinds of kin networks are invisible to the established hierarchies, "the cross-generational production of Black queer social life" (Shange 2019: 47) nevertheless provides possibility for Black trans subjects navigating violent systems. This possibility looks like connections that are based not on reproductive or biological relationships but on a sense of love, support, and enduring solidarity for one another.

The possibility that these connections provide is not just for those youn-ger folks, like Mock. For Black queer and trans elders, the process of building intergenerational kinship bonds can serve as a movement of return. Savannah Shange (2019: 50) highlights the possibility that these kinds of connections offer while reflecting on the bonds she and her students built: "The fullness of the moment sent me back through the wormhole to my own adolescence, and I felt the bite of how badly I needed a space like the one we co-created." For some elders, the process of building intergenerational kinship bonds—of making a path, a way—for those who come after provides an opportunity to build a space they didn't have.

Mock's description captures two points that characterize this form of intergenerational kinship bond. First, this bond provides a sense of mentorship/ "femmetorship" made possible because these older women had navigated similar experiences themselves. The knowledge these women bestowed via resources, advice, and perspective helped guide Mock through an uncertain period in her life. Second, this bond across age provides a knowledge of the past. This sense of connection to one's history is characterized by Mock's description of a longer tradition of trans women in her community. This deep legacy is exemplified by Black trans activist Raquel Willis's (2018) characterization of Sylvia Rivera as her "transcestor."[2] Willis names and Mock describes the particular intergenerational connection they have to those trans femmes of color who have gone before them, those who felt it necessary to pass their resources and knowledge on to folks like Mock and Willis who would come up after them.

On another level, Mock illustrates intergenerational kinship by describing her resource network as an underground railroad. This use of metaphor connects her experience to enslaved Black ancestors navigating along secret routes through safe houses, churches, and attics to move from bondage toward freedom. Like her ancestors, Mock reached freedom through the underground network that "gui-ded" her, like the North Star, through uncertain times. Mock describes this process of seeking freedom with help from others as gaining "an agency that empowered me to take my life, my body, and my being into my own hands." Perhaps her ancestors would have described their process similarly. In both cases, these net-works are able to materialize and endure only through a reliance on and trust in one another. This kind of crossing embodies the fugitive movement of Blackness/transness at the boundaries of normativity.

In this same section of the memoir, Mock recalls the beginning of her medical transition as a teen, alongside her best friend, Wendi, whom she describes as her sister. Mock's description in this passage, in line with Langer's (2014: 66) discussion of the "collective experience of transition," highlights the ways that the sharing of medical information and resources can function as both practices of kinship building and communal construction. Mock (2014c: 135) writes,

When she graduated to Estradiol injections weeks later, Wendi passed her Pre-marin bottles to me. She claimed she didn't like the pills because they bloated her, but I knew part of her didn't want to go on the journey alone. When I think of this time with Wendi, I'm reminded of the line from Toni Morrison's *Sula*: "Nobody was minding us, so we minded ourselves." I was her sister, and she didn't want to leave me behind. We needed each other to create who we were supposed to be.

Mock's juxtaposed descriptions of her relationship with Wendi and with these older trans women highlight various forms of kinship bonds that can emerge within the t4t framework. Not only does she forge a bond with someone—a sister—who is also transitioning, but she also enters a kin network with older trans women who have already transitioned and are able to pass on their knowledge.

In this passage, Mock links textual kinship to her process of forging kin bonds with Wendi. It's certainly no coincidence that Mock quotes *Sula* (Morrison 1973), a text that has been central to Black lesbian feminist literary critique since it came out in the early 1970s. Barbara Smith's 1978 piece, "Toward a Black Feminist Criticism," most famously argues that "Morrison's work poses both lesbian and feminist questions about Black women's autonomy and their impact on each other's lives" (23). Mock's use of *Sula* highlights her relationship to Wendi, and her textual kinship to *Sula*, through a moment of recognition in the text. Just as Nel and Sula grow up together, their deep friendship being central to the people they grow to become, Janet's and Wendi's tandem transitions are not simply simultaneous medical procedures but a journey undertaken by two sisters.

Smith writes of Sula and Nel's bond, "The knowledge that 'they were neither white nor male' is the inherent explanation of their need for each other. Morrison depicts in literature the necessary bonding that has always taken place between Black women for the sake of barest survival. Together the two girls can find the courage to create themselves" (24). Smith's use of *need* is critical here because it parallels Mock's use in her own description of her sisterhood with Wendi. Smith's analysis of Nel and Sula's mutual co-construction could just as easily describe the process of Black trans becoming that emerges from Janet and Wendi's kinship bonds. Smith frames "the two girls . . . creat[ing] themselves" within a broader context, highlighting the racialized and gendered preconditions and implications of their kinship. It is in this context that Smith emphasizes just how important Nel and Sula's connection is to their collective creation. This is why a Black feminist intervention in trans studies is so critical. Without it, both the significance of Mock and Wendi's bond, and the connections to a genealogy of Black feminist thought, are elided. This genealogy includes Morrison's *Sula* and the reflection of self that it provided for Mock, as well as Smith's illustration of the racialized and gendered implications of Morrison's representations. A Black feminist analysis of the memoir recognizes the significance of these connections. This "necessary bonding" that Wendi and Janet have undertaken is, in fact, part of a longer tradition of ancestors, something "that has always taken place between Black women."

Conclusion

The concept of self-making, and the term *self-made man* in particular, have been taken up in various forms of reclamation and disidentification within the trans community (McBee 2012; Rubin 2003). The language of self-making has served to capture experiences of self-determination, to highlight a sense of autonomy in the face of ostensibly predetermined forces, and even to describe the financial burden of medical transition.[3] Still, the self-made man's connections to capitalism and the American Dream might serve to reinforce "a normative masculinity mediated by neoliberal socio-economic relations" (Irving 2009: 376).

In this article, I have approached the concept of transness from a different perspective, meditating on transness as a communal practice rather than a process of self-making. As the three previous sections have illustrated, a Black feminist approach underscores the importance of the collective in the construction of the self. Utilizing *trans* as "a term of relationality" (Halberstam 2005: 49), I have sought to illustrate the ways that trans people emerge more fully into themselves through the help of multiple kinds of bonds. Here, *trans* has represented the movement of self in relation to others. The bonds that we make move us forward, they return us to our history, they take us somewhere else completely.

As the field of Black trans studies emerges, scholars are beginning to examine the relationships between transness and Blackness (Bey 2017), movement (Silva Santana 2017), and movements (Green and Ellison 2014), to name a few. This article has built on and furthered some of these claims, exploring trans (studies, texts, and identity formation) in relationship to Black (-ness, feminist thought). Using t4t grounded in Black feminism as a framework, I have highlighted the various relations between Black feminist thought and trans studies, between texts and Black trans readers, and between Black feminism and Black trans emergence, illustrating the centrality of these kinship bonds to the process of collective construction. Describing the relational nature of trans using kinship language is fraught, given that the concept of family holds its own historical baggage (Shange 2019: 44). The work that I do here seeks to imagine a way forward. At its best, the kind of co-construction that I have described might be a practice in reciprocity, "a mutually beneficial site of Black praxis" (49).

Mock's use of *Sula* to describe her sisterhood with Wendi emphasizes the centrality of connection in creating a collective sense of self that I have sought to describe in this article. Seeing ourselves as part of a longer history and creating connections with others who help us imagine otherwise are important aspects of constructing and maintaining a robust sense of self. Simply put, we cannot make ourselves without the help of others. The same might be true for the field of trans studies. This help might come through forging strange kinships across difference. Black trans studies models this, drawing on those who have come before in the hope of offering something for those to come. This movement of return to the work of Black feminist thought provides a different, collective approach for the field of trans studies moving forward. Following Mock's lead, we might recognize just how much we need each other to create who we're supposed to be.

Amira Lundy-Harris is a PhD candidate in the Harriet Tubman Department of Women, Gender, and Sexuality Studies at the University of Maryland, College Park.

Notes

1. In "Olympia's Maid: Reclaiming Black Female Subjectivity," Black feminist artist and critic Lorraine O'Grady (2009: 318) deftly illustrates the implications of ungendered Black female flesh when she writes, "The female body in the West is not a unitary sign. Rather, like a coin, it has an obverse and a reverse: on the one side, it is white; on the other, nonwhite or, prototypically, black. The two bodies cannot be separated, nor can one body be understood in isolation from the other in the West's metaphoric construction of 'woman.' White is what woman is; not-white (and the stereotypes that not-white gathers in) is what she had better not be."

2. "July 2, 1951: Transcestor Sylvia Rivera was born with a fighter's spirit that would galvanize the much maligned trans community. She was a true radical in every sense—calling out transphobia, capitalism, white supremacy, militarism, assimilation and more. Thank you, Mama!"

3. "In the tradition of the American idealism of the individual and the refusal of most insurance policies to cover trans* health care, trans* persons create their own path with their own money" (Langer 2014: 71).

References

Aiken, Joshua, Jessica Marion Modi, and Olivia R. Polk. 2020. "Issued by Way of 'The Issue of Blackness.'" *TSQ* 7, no. 3: 427–44.

Allen, Jafari S. 2012. "Black/Queer/Diaspora at the Current Conjuncture." *GLQ* 18, no. 2: 211–48.

Bey, Marquis. 2017. "The Trans*-ness of Blackness, the Blackness of Trans*-ness." In "The Issue of Blackness," edited by Treva Ellison, Kai M. Green, Matt Richardson, and C. Riley Snorton. Special issue, *TSQ* 4, no. 2: 275–95.

Chaudhry, V Varun. 2019. "Trans/Coalitional Love-Politics: Black Feminisms and the Radical Possibilities of Transgender Studies." *TSQ* 6, no. 4: 521–38.

Christian, Barbara. 1988. "The Race for Theory." *Feminist Studies* 14, no. 1: 67–79.

Cohen, Cathy. 1997. "Punks, Bulldaggers, and Welfare Queens: The Radical Potential of Queer Politics?" *GLQ* 3, no. 4: 437–65.

Craft, William, and Ellen Craft. (1860) 1999. *Running a Thousand Miles for Freedom; or, The Escape of William and Ellen Craft from Slavery.* Charlottesville: University of Virginia Libraries.

Dame, Avery. 2017. "Talk amongst Yourselves: 'Community' in Transgender Counterpublic Discourse Online, 1990–2014." PhD diss., University of Maryland, College Park.

Eastwood, Alexander. 2014. "How, Then, Might the Transsexual Read? Notes toward a Trans Literary History." *TSQ* 1, no. 4: 590–604.

Ellison, Ralph. 1952. *Invisible Man.* New York: Random House.

Ellison, Treva, Kai M. Green, Matt Richardson, and C. Riley Snorton. 2017. "We Got Issues: Toward a Black Trans*/Studies." In "The Issue of Blackness," edited by Treva Ellison, Kai M. Green, Matt Richardson, and C. Riley Snorton. Special issue, *TSQ* 4, no. 2: 162–69.

Green, Kai M., and Marquis Bey. 2017. "Where Black Feminist Thought and Trans* Feminism Meet: A Conversation." *Souls* 19, no. 4: 438–54.

Green, Kai M., and Treva Ellison. 2014. "Tranifest." *TSQ* 1, nos. 1–2: 222–24.

Halberstam, Jack. 2005. *In a Queer Time and Place: Transgender Bodies, Subcultural Lives.* New York: New York University Press.

Hammonds, Evelynn M. 1997. "Toward a Genealogy of Black Female Sexuality: The Problematic of Silence." In *Feminist Genealogies, Colonial Legacies, Democratic Futures,* edited by M. Jacqui Alexander and Chandra Talpade Mohanty, 170–82. New York: Routledge.

Harris-Perry, Melissa V. 2011. *Sister Citizen: Shame, Stereotypes, and Black Women in America.* New Haven, CT: Yale University Press.

Harris-Perry, Melissa. 2014. "Trans activist: 'Not Enough of Our Stories Are Being Told.'" MSNBC, February 1. www.msnbc.com/melissa-harris-perry/watch/not-enough-of-our-stories-are-being-told-133656643761.

Hurston, Zora Neale. 1937. *Their Eyes Were Watching God.* Philadelphia: J. B. Lippincott.

Irving, Dan. 2009. "The Self-Made Trans Man as Risky Business: A Critical Examination of Gaining Recognition for Trans Rights through Economic Discourse." *Temple Law Review* 18, no. 2: 375–96.

Kolker, Jeanne. 2014. "Q&A: Janet Mock on Getting Real." *Wisconsin State Journal,* April 14. madison.com/entertainment/arts_and_theatre/books/q-a-janet-mock-on-getting-real/article_77a2339b-8855-5369-bb6c-18b2cb67d772.html.

Langer, SJ. 2014. "Our Body Project: From Mourning to Creating the Transgender Body." *International Journal of Transgenderism* 15, no. 2: 66–75.

McBee, Thomas Page. 2012. "The Truck Stop." Self-Made Man #1, *Rumpus,* February 21. therumpus.net/2012/02/self-made-man-1-the-truckstop/.

McMillan, Terry. 1992. *Waiting to Exhale.* New York: Viking.

Mock, Janet. 2014a. "Janet Mock on Words and Redefining Realness." January 30. YouTube video, 1:56. www.youtube.com/watch?v=cNQ3302H3BU.

Mock, Janet. 2014b. *Piers Morgan Live.* Interview by Piers Morgan. CNN, February 5. www.youtube.com/watch?v=oF8WiuxYoE4.

Mock, Janet. 2014c. *Redefining Realness: My Path to Womanhood, Identity, Love, and So Much More.* New York: Atria.

Mock, Janet. 2017. "Dear Men of 'The Breakfast Club': Trans Women Aren't a Prop, Ploy, or Sexual Predators." *Allure,* July 31. www.allure.com/story/janet-mock-response-the-breakfast-club-trans-women.

Morrison, Toni. 1973. *Sula.* New York: Knopf.

Muñoz, José Esteban. 1999. *Disidentifications: Queers of Color and the Performance of Politics.* Minneapolis: University of Minnesota Press.

Muñoz, José Esteban. 2009. *Cruising Utopia: The Then and There of Queer Futurity.* New York: New York University Press.

O'Grady, Lorraine. 2009. "Olympia's Maid: Reclaiming Black Female Subjectivity." In *Still Brave: The Evolution of Black Women's Studies,* edited by Stanlie M. James, Frances Smith Foster, and Beverly Guy-Sheftall, 318–35. New York: Feminist Press.

Roberts, Neil. 2015. *Freedom as Marronage.* Chicago: University of Chicago Press.

Rubin, Henry. 2003. *Self-Made Men: Identity and Embodiment among Transsexual Men.* Nashville: Vanderbilt University Press.

Shange, Savannah. 2019. "Play Aunties and Dyke Bitches: Gender, Generation, and the Ethics of Black Queer Kinship." *Black Scholar* 49, no. 1: 40–54.

Sharpe, Christina. 2016. *In the Wake: On Blackness and Being.* Durham, NC: Duke University Press.

Silva Santana, Dora. 2017. "Transitionings and Returnings: Experiments with the Poetics of Transatlantic Water." In "The Issue of Blackness," edited by Treva Ellison, Kai M. Green, Matt Richardson, and C. Riley Snorton. Special issue, *TSQ* 4, no. 2: 181–90.

Smith, Barbara. 1978. "Toward a Black Feminist Criticism." *Radical Teacher,* no. 7: 20–27.

Snorton, C. Riley. 2017. *Black on Both Sides: A Racial History of Trans Identity.* Minneapolis: University of Minnesota Press.

Spillers, Hortense J. 1987. "Mama's Baby, Papa's Maybe: An American Grammar Book." *Diacritics* 17, no. 2: 65–81.

Stone, Sandy. 1992. "The *Empire* Strikes Back: A Posttranssexual Manifesto." *Camera Obscura,* no. 29: 150–76.

The New School. 2014a. "bell hooks and Laverne Cox in a Public Dialogue at The New School." October 13. YouTube video, 1:36:08. www.youtube.com/watch?v=9oMmZIJijgY.

The New School. 2014b. "bell hooks—Are You Still a Slave? Liberating the Black Female Body | Eugene Lang College." May 7. YouTube video, 1:55:32. www.youtube.com/watch?v=rJko hNROvzs.

Tinsley, Omise'eke Natasha. 2008. "Black Atlantic, Queer Atlantic: Queer Imaginings of the Middle Passage." *GLQ* 14, nos. 2–3: 191–215.

Tinsley, Omise'eke Natasha. 2012. "Extract from 'Water, Shoulders, into the Black Pacific.'" *GLQ* 18, nos. 2–3: 263–76.

Walker, Alice. 1975. "In Search of Zora Neale Hurston." *Ms.,* March, 74–89.

Willis, Raquel (@RaquelWillis_). 2018. "July 2, 1951: Transcestor Sylvia Rivera was born with a fighter's spirit that would galvanize the much maligned trans community." Twitter, July 2, 9:06 a.m. twitter.com/RaquelWillis_/status/1013816206703423488.

T4t Love-Politics

Monica Roberts's TransGriot *and Love as a Theory of Justice*

V. JO HSU

Abstract This essay considers Monica Roberts's long-standing blog, *TransGriot*, as a model of T4t love-politics. Drawing from Jennifer Nash's work on Black feminism, the author argues that *TransGriot* centers interpersonal and intra- and intercommunal relationships as driving forces of social and systemic change. This approach to t4t enabled Roberts to center trans voices, trans needs, and trans thriving while also demanding accountability from all communities that intersect with the lives of Black trans women. What emerges is an understanding of justice as built and sustained by the difficult work of relating—of making ourselves vulnerable to, and bearing witness to, one another.
Keywords Black feminism, intersectionality, t4t, storytelling, *TransGriot*

> We Black trans women are walking examples of intersectionality. We are an unde-
> niable part of the Black community. We are part of the TBLGQ one. We are part of
> the Black SGL community. We are trailblazing women doing our part to uplift
> all the communities we intersect and interact with."
> —Monica Roberts, *TransGriot*

The word *blog* seems insufficient in capturing the pathbreaking legacy of Monica Roberts's *TransGriot*. For nearly fifteen years, the website provided a lifeline of trans history and activism. As a Black trans woman, Roberts wrote with tremendous care for her communities while holding them accountable to their most vulnerable members. She chronicled the losses, triumphs, and struggles of Black and trans—and particularly Black trans—people while providing political commentary and advocacy. Throughout her writing, she pointed to the intersectional wisdom and leadership of Black trans women. Their experiences at the nexus of gender- and race-based oppressions illuminate the interrelations of these struggles as well as the imperative that movements for racial justice, gender equality, and TBLGQ[1] liberation work in relationship with one another.

After Roberts's sudden passing in 2020, members of her widespread communities reflected on the extent of her impact. Writer and Hollywood icon Janet Mock (2020) credits *TransGriot* as a space "where I learned about our long and deep history as Black trans folks." Established in 2006, *TransGriot* was named for the West African storytellers who served as "a visible and tangible human link to the past" (Roberts 2006c). Roberts used storytelling to thread together a vast array of trans experiences past and present. This through-line of trans history became "the gateway for countless people's journey to their gender identity" (Raquel Willis quoted in Kurutz 2020), inviting them into a lineage of gender-variant people across centuries and geographies.

In drawing these connections, Roberts never shied away from intra- and intercommunal conflict. She approached community as a verb—as ongoing labor that requires thought, reflexivity, and the creation and maintenance of responsive infrastructures. "It's time for us to organize," she wrote to other Black trans people in 2008, proposing a national and global network of African American trans sisterhood (Roberts 2008b). She reiterated her charge in 2011, emphasizing the need for bridges between trans and cis Black communities: "We need to be talking to our people about who we are as trans people of African descent and getting them to realize that Black transgender problems are Black community problems" (Roberts 2011c). Likewise, she consistently challenged racism within trans and queer communities, noting how Black trans folks are "dismissed or vilified" within TBLGQ circles (Roberts 2007d). She demanded that trans, queer, feminist, and Black organizations recognize the mutuality of their struggles as well as the intersectionality of their constituents. Her writing then modeled discursive and affective strategies for reshaping our communities toward mutually supportive and intersectional politics. Latoya Roberts (2020), Monica's sister, wrote that Monica "left a blueprint for others to show how it's done." In this essay, I retrace *Trans-Griot* as a blueprint for t4t love-politics—a transformational care based in openness toward and responsibility for one another.

To my knowledge, Roberts never used the term *t4t* in her work, but she wrote in the spirit of such trans care. Her work often exemplifies what Hil Malatino names a "t4t praxis of love," which prioritizes trans community while also acknowledging that trans people frequently make things harder for one another. In Malatino's (2019: 656) words, this practice, "dwells in difficulty. . . . It is about being with and bearing with; about witnessing one another." Roberts's approach to this often-fraught relationality aligns closely with Jennifer Nash's (2013: 2) Black feminist love-politics—a politics that "transform[s] love from the personal . . . into a theory of justice." Love-politics centers affective connections as a site of community

building and political transformation. It requires "expansive conceptions of relationality, encouraging us to view ourselves as deeply embedded in the world, and
thus as deeply connected to others" (Nash 2019: 117). My priority then, in addition to highlighting Monica Roberts's teachings for present and future trans orga-
nizers, is to situate her within a broader lineage of t4t politics as well as Black
feminist theory.[2] *TransGriot* and Roberts's life work provide models for and insight
into what V Varun Chaudhry (2019) names a "trans/coalitional love-politics"—a
critical orientation, rooted in the structural precarity of Black womanhood (trans
and cis), that grapples with the complex entanglements of racial, gender, and
sexual oppressions.

To better parse the efficacy of *TransGriot*'s t4t world making, I draw from
Nash's theorization of love-politics. According to Nash (2019: 116), Black feminist love-politics centers two key ideas: witnessing and vulnerability. The former
"describes black feminist theory's investment in a rich and political counterhistory." Witnessing involves "calculated self-disclosure that puts political pressure on the host of ways that violence inflicted on black women's bodies is rendered normative or invisible" (120). *TransGriot*, in providing a platform for Black
trans women to voice their experiences, exposed the social and structural conditions that enable transmisogynoir (see Krell 2017). Often, it emphasized the
complicities of trans communities, Black communities, and other collectives with
which Black transgender lives intersect. In exposing these collusions, *TransGriot*
demands more of Black trans women's affective relations, calling for a reciprocal
care that can nurture visionary political futures.

TransGriot's deliberately intersectional politics arose from Roberts's own
experience, in which "my being Black goes wherever I do and is part and parcel
of whatever community I interact with" (Roberts 2012a). Often dismayed at the
single-issue focus of both Black communities and trans communities, Roberts
sought to highlight the overlapping concerns and inescapable interdependence
of those marginalized by white heteropatriarchy (see Spillers 1987; Snorton 2017;
Green and Bey 2017; Ellison et al. 2017). On her blog, Roberts linked her embodied
insights with those of other Black trans folks, people of color, and TBLGQ folks.
She pursued the mutual vulnerability at the heart of Nash's love-politics: an openness to being bound up with one another, and to being wounded and affected
by one another. *TransGriot*, as both a media platform and virtual gathering
space that centered trans people, fostered a t4t love-politics deeply attuned to
the politics of intimacy—how the range and limitations of our care participate in
circulations of power. The blog envisions and demands trans communities that
are more inclusive of race and class, TLBGQ communities that foreground Black
transgender experiences, and Black communities willing to fight for their trans
and queer kin.

T4t Witnessing and Vulnerability

Consistently updated between 2006 and Roberts's passing in 2020, *TransGriot* archives a sweeping history of trans experiences. The immediacy of this platform enabled Roberts to respond to breaking news and trans issues in real time. Though *TransGriot* covered a plethora of subjects, from popular media to local and national elections to Roberts's National Football League draft picks, it is probably best known for its coverage of transphobic violence and its role in holding media outlets accountable in their reportage. Often positioned in direct opposition to mass media accounts, *TransGriot* provided a check on news outlets in their gross mishandling of trans stories. It exposed journalistic complicity in anti-trans violence and modeled more thoughtful approaches to trans stories. This digital space created necessary shelter so that trans folks could bear witness to their experiences. More, in leveraging her resources to protect, uplift, and celebrate her trans kin, Roberts modeled and demanded better from cisgender allies.

In the blog's first year, Roberts responded to an Associated Press (AP) article about a transgender student in Gary, Indiana, who was turned away from her high school prom. Roberts notes that the AP continually misgendered Kevin Logan, although she had "spent years defining and exploring her gender identity" (Roberts 2006b). Roberts (2006b) rewrote the AP's article with the correct pronouns and appended the *AP Stylebook*'s guidelines for stories on transgender people:

> transgender: *Use the pronoun preferred by the individuals who have acquired the physical characteristics of the opposite sex or present themselves in a way that does not correspond with their sex at birth.*
>
> **If that preference is not expressed, use the pronoun consistent with the way the individuals live publicly.**

This passage reappears in Roberts's subsequent posts titled "Can't Y'all Read Your Own Stylebooks" (Roberts 2007c) and "I Repeat: Can't Y'all Read Your Own Stylebooks" (Roberts 2008d) in which Roberts expresses continued frustration with reporters' willful ignorance. Calling attention to the AP's violation of their own policies, Roberts reveals how lazy or indifferent reportage facilitates a broader culture that denigrates and endangers transgender people.

Over the next year, Roberts became more direct in her critiques of journalistic complicity. In July of 2008, she rewrote the story of Ebony Whitaker, who was described in major news outlets as a "transgendered prostitute" (WMC Action News 5 2008). These stories consistently referred to Whitaker as a man who "was dressed as a woman when he was found shot to death." Reporters also used Whitaker's deadname, which, Roberts points out, many trans folks do not even share with friends or loved ones (Ajani 2020). Beyond the blatant disregard of such misgendering, such irresponsible journalism also delays or misleads investigations. In contrast, Roberts (2008c) restored Ebony's name and described her as "a beautiful young African-American woman, with reddish streaks in her long blonde hair, arched brows, perfectly applied eyeshadow and lip liner. In a comment on her own post, Roberts reflects on how familial rejection and employment discrimination participated in Ebony's victimization, connecting this singular event to structured vulnerabilities. When Ebony could no longer speak her truth, Roberts stepped into the role of witness, "draw[ing] on memory . . . to demand an ethical reckoning" (Nash 2019: 116) with the events that precipitated Ebony's murder.

Two weeks later, Roberts built on that ethical imperative with the story of Angie Zapata, who was deadnamed and misgendered in the *Greeley Tribune*. As she did with Whitaker's story, Roberts rewrote the article on Zapata "to show you what a properly written story on a transgender person following the AP Stylebook guidelines should look like" (Roberts 2008a). This time, other news outlets picked up *TransGriot*'s version. After a blogger at *Blabbeando* amplified Roberts's rewrite, the AP's original reporter printed an acknowledgment of his mistake, and ABC News revised their own post about the murder (Duque 2008). In a subsequent post, Roberts (2008e) reflects on the sequence of events—how speaking out "got results." Addressing critics who characterized her blog as "angry," Roberts asks, "If I hadn't wrote the blog post . . . , would the story actually be getting legs in the media or the blogosphere, much less the mea culpa story in the Greeley Tribune later that day?" (Roberts 2008e). This series of events established momentum for *TransGriot*, which practiced its vehement truth telling not only as counterhistory but also as a means of communing and building collective power.

As *TransGriot* garnered global attention, Roberts regularly spotlighted trans leaders both domestic and abroad. She signal-boosted other writers such as Mia Nikasimo, who discussed trans experiences as a Nigerian in diaspora (Roberts 2012c), and Juliet Victor Mukasa (2006), the chairperson of Sexual Minorities Uganda. These posts frequently stressed a core principle of Black feminist witnessing: that Black women "can see and even name forms of violence that other subjects cannot see, or simply refuse to see" (Nash 2019: 119). Black women's social location, which positions them at the intersection of anti-Blackness and misogyny, also gives them particularly sharp insight into the mechanisms that institutionalize those prejudices. During the 2012 push for marriage equality, Roberts (2012d) echoed Aisha Moodie-Mills's research on Black trans and gay experiences—noting how, despite celebratory narratives of LGBTQ progress in recent years, "the quality of life of many black gay and transgender people remained relatively unchanged." The "headline policy priorities" of well-funded gay movements, in other words, did little for those targeted by gross disparities in income, educational attainment, housing security, and healthcare (Roberts 2012a). By contrast, a trans and queer liberation rooted in Moodie-Mills's proposals—with inclusive family policies and safety-net programs, funding for transgender and gay entrepreneurs, and audits of school discipline policies—would increase opportunities and life chances for the TBLGQ community more broadly.

In bringing together this range of trans perspectives, Roberts demonstrated the vast scope of transgender experience while continually centering those most affected by structured inequities. Her t4t care reached across racial, national, and other social boundaries in pursuit of Black feminist vulnerability—that is, a "commitment to be intimately bound to the other (or to others)" (Nash 2019: 116). Roberts's frequent critiques of racism in TBLGQ spaces, trans and queerphobia in people of color (POC) spaces, US centrism in Western spaces, and classism and colorism in trans spaces model a sort of "tough-love" in love-politics. In each case, she stresses that trans, queer, and POC "survivals are mutually dependent" (Nash 2019). She demands that her widespread communities do better by one another in pursuit of mutually desirable futures. As in Nash's theorization of vulnerability, Roberts's vulnerability is not just about the potential to be injured but also about the transformative potential of being open to others—about how we change when we see ourselves as acting within and accountable to a whole much larger than ourselves.

The urgency with which Roberts writes about t4t vulnerability becomes most apparent in her direct address to other Black trans women. In a post about colorism, Roberts calls attention to how white beauty norms still infiltrate and divide Black trans circles. She pivots attention away from interpersonal differences, insisting, "We have far more serious issues to tackle," including "crushing unemployment/underemployment, off the charts antitrans violence aimed at our Black transwomen, lack of media visibility, a fundamental misunderstanding of what trans is in the cis and SGL African-American communities and a six decade old trans narrative in the parent culture that is overwhelmingly stacked toward telling the stories of our white trans counterparts" (Roberts 2013b). These issues remain central throughout Roberts's blogging: employment discrimination, under- and misrepresentation, and widespread hostility to and/or neglect of Black trans women within their supposed communities. Enforcing hierarchies of skin tone and hair color, Roberts (2013b) tells her readers, ignores the fact that "we are all Black and we are **ALL** hated for it." These distractions ultimately reinforce the hold of white supremacy, preventing concerted efforts to change the structural, historical, and social conditions that imperil Black trans lives. In Roberts's (2013b) words, Black trans women have far "bigger civil rights prizes" to pursue, and "we cannot afford to have in chocolate Trans World colorism dividing us."

Building from the micro to the macro, Roberts expanded her calls for mutual vulnerability to larger communities whose fates are bound up with those of Black trans women—including transgender people more broadly. For example, when a reader attacked one of Roberts's posts about the specific challenges faced by trans women of color, Roberts responded with "Race and Class Still Matter in the Trans Community." In this follow-up post, Roberts addresses her critic—Jacqueline, who identifies as a white trans woman—by spotlighting the contradictions of color-evasive inclusion. Jacqueline accuses Roberts of being "divisive," but Roberts points out that she cannot divide what was never united. In most trans circles, Roberts (2013c) writes, "[Black trans women] are invisible because you not only refuse to see and hear me, you refuse to acknowledge our existence." Without "honest discussion about race and class issues and how they affect the trans community," community itself is impossible (Roberts 2013c). Instead, white trans people continue to benefit from the labor of advocates such as Roberts herself while the particular needs, desires, and experiences of Black trans women remain unaddressed.

When Roberts writes about "the trans community," the phrase is in some way aspirational—a call for accomplices to build a Trans World-that-could-be by directly addressing all the intragroup impediments to such collaborations. In a more recent example, written as an address to "Trans World," Roberts (2018d) targets trans supporters of SESTA (Stop Enabling Sex Traffickers Act). Roberts expresses her ire at "sanctimonious comments from the trans peanut gallery cheering that [sex workers] need to 'get a real job.'" Echoing Mock, Roberts first affirms that "sex work is work" before highlighting the rampant employment discrimination that channels trans people disproportionately into sex work. SESTA, Roberts points out, colludes with these mechanisms of disenfranchisement by shutting down digital platforms used to reach, vet, and select clients. After issuing this reprimand, however, Roberts returns to the hope of trans solidarity, reminding readers that "the folks who engage in sex work are still and will always be your trans family." Rather than derogating some of the most vulnerable members of Trans World, trans folks should "save that derision for the people who gleefully oppress us." As in her response to Jacqueline, Roberts directs her criticism toward the specific goal of strengthening and protecting trans communities, which cannot be accomplished without first addressing the discriminatory attitudes that cleave those communities.

Vulnerability beyond Trans World

Monica Roberts's vulnerability logic extends to the other communities to which she belongs, including TBLGQ collectives, Black communities, and other grassroots and professional organizations. She used her position as an insider to demand accountability from these groups. As a member of the National Association of

LGBTQ Journalists (NLGJA), Roberts (2018b) decried the organization's "overwhelmingly cis white gay" focus. At the 2018 convention, where emcee Marshall McPeek greeted attendees as "Ladies and gentlemen, things and its," Roberts yelled out, "Oh no he did not. There are no things or its here" (Birnbaum 2018). Throughout the subsequent deliberation among TBLGQ journalists, Roberts repeatedly situated herself as a member of the community demanding more of her colleagues and her profession. In her first *TransGriot* post on the matter, Roberts (2018b) addresses McPeek directly:

> No, Mr. McPeek and by extension, NLGJA and FOX News, there were no 'things and its' in that Hotel Zoso room that September 8 night. There were trans, gender non-conforming (GNC) and non-binary (NB) people in there. There were your trans, GNC, and NB media colleagues in that room. Most importantly there were your trans, NB, and GNC identified journalism students in that audience who are aspiring to and working diligently towards getting to the level where you are.

Roberts's critique hinges on her and McPeek sharing this heterogenous community, with its unequal distributions of power. McPeek's thoughtless address was particularly harmful because of his status as a recognized leader in the NLGJA and because younger trans, NB, and GNC journalists may look to him as an example. While some rushed to defend McPeek's attempted gag as one with "no reference to gender identity" (Friess 2018), Roberts emphasized context over intent. Regardless of whether McPeek imagined trans folks as the referent of his "things and its," he was speaking to, and as an authoritative figure of, an organization "dedicated to ensuring accurate and respectful coverage of the TBLGQ community" (Roberts 2018b). Such thoughtless word choice, in addition to alienating trans and gender-nonconforming journalists, also perpetuates the transphobic discourse that pervades mass media—a problem *TransGriot* actively combatted throughout its many years.

   Roberts made these connections more explicit when another cis gay journalist, Steve Friess, penned a furious defense of McPeek for the *Bay Area Reporter*. Friess (2018) accused "pitchfork-wielding trans Twitter" of overreacting and needlessly attacking an "LGBTQ pioneer." Roberts's answer was unapologetic. She draws a direct line between McPeek's rhetoric and the violence targeting trans women. This is "a time when trans, NB, and GNC community is under legislative assault and their humanity is under attack by the Republican Party, trans exterminationalist radical 'feminists' and the conservative movement" (Roberts 2018b). McPeek, Friess, and their supporters are aligning themselves with these groups and their antitrans, antiqueer agendas. If the NLGJA "think[s] it's okay to call trans people 'things and its,'" Roberts writes, "what hope do we trans folks [have] of getting respectful coverage from mainstream media, much less have NLGJA stand up for us when the inevitable misgendering or facts free anti-trans reporting happens?" (Roberts 2018c). Roberts's question, which calls for the NLGJA to honor its own stated mission, demonstrates that she's not swinging pitchforks for the sake of antagonism. Rather, she is sharing the hard truths required of mutual vulnerability, calling on TBLGQ groups to recognize and redress the forms of harm that pervade their own spaces.

By bearing witness to oft-occluded experiences from within communities, Black feminist love-politics encourages people "to ask about our deep responsibilities to each other" (Nash 2019: 117). Roberts's vehement advocacy as a member of the NLGJA positions trans experiences and thus trans pain as integral to the NLGJA's membership. She situates these wounds in "intimate proximity" (117) to cisgender reporters, and she queries about the role and responsibility of NLGJA in a moment when trans people are actively persecuted by government agencies and right-wing movements. These are, of course, parties whose platforms espouse attitudes and aspirations contrary to queer lives. Outlining the broader social and political stakes, Roberts pressures NLGJA members and leadership to consider how their lives are bound up with those of trans people, and what responsibilities follow from that proximity.

Roberts exercises similar rhetorical turns when addressing her other communities, taking particular care to spotlight Black trans issues as integral to Black concerns. Here too, Roberts focuses her attention on the systemic—how her Black relations are subjected to many of the same mechanisms of discrimination that target trans people. In 2008 she identified the most pressing concern as economic disenfranchisement and mapped how Black, trans, and Black trans people are denied equal opportunity for employment. If trans people are both "[cut] off from legitimate employment *and* the love and support of their family," Roberts (2008f) reasons, some will "[feel] they have no other option but to turn tricks for cash. The end result of that can be what happened to young Ebony Whitaker a few weeks ago." As she did when addressing the NLGJA, she demonstrates how families of origin can participate in the marginalization and abuse of transgender people. The frequent abandonment of transgender people to underground economies, Roberts points out, makes them even more vulnerable to police violence—an undeniable concern for Black communities. Black trans people, Roberts (2008f) emphasizes, "want to do our part to help. But this is a two-way road of mutual assistance. You have a moral obligation as fellow African-Americans to help us, too."

Love-Politics as Groundwork for Transformation

For all the pressure that Roberts put on her people to do better by one another, *TransGriot* expends just as much time and effort facilitating and celebrating collective victories. In doing so, it frames collective care as a necessary precondition to political agitation. Archiving fourteen years of trans memory, the blog is both a record of and an active participant in the growth of trans political power and media influence. Roberts began following Andrea Jenkins's career in 2012, three years before Jenkins became the first African American transgender woman elected to a major city council. When Jenkins's campaign for Congress began in earnest, *TransGriot* became a fierce advocate for her, emphasizing how important it is to have trans people in positions to "formulate public policy for their constituents and our community" (Roberts 2016a; 2017a). While similar arguments were made in other trans- and queer-affirming spaces, *TransGriot*'s advocacy was especially powerful in that readers already had years of familiarity with Jenkins's work.

On *TransGriot*, Jenkins was more than a political candidate. Readers had already known her as a published poet and as curator of the University of Minnesota's Transgender Oral History Project. She was a "tennis loving homegirl" who led a "Creating Change" seminar about interracial trans sisterhood and who roomed with Roberts at the "TransFaith of Color Conference" (Roberts 2014, 2015). After Jenkins's groundbreaking victory, Roberts channeled the support of her readers to organizations that had helped secure this win. When soliciting donations for the Trans United Fund, Roberts (2017e) was able to point to their track record of "getting our people elected, like Minneapolis councilmembers elect Andrea Jenkins and Phillipe Cunningham." The continuity of Roberts's narration both outlined and helped actuate trans political influence.

Similarly, Roberts's support of trans artists and media built on her extant relationships and her long history of cultivating Black trans consciousness. In the first year of the blog, she lamented the dearth of Black trans representation, imagining a version of the Oscar-nominated *Transamerica* that could capture the complexity and richness of Black trans life (Roberts 2006a). The next year, she followed up with an overview of the limited and limiting representations of Black transgender TV characters (Roberts 2007b). She continued to track this problem through posts such as "Hollywood Is as Important to Trans People as Washington DC" and "Hey Hollywood, Trans Actors Exist, So Hire Them!" (Roberts 2011a, 2016b). To secure thoughtful trans representation, Roberts (2006a) wrote presciently, "we'd probably have to write, produce, and direct it ourselves." When *Pose* arrived in 2018, promising just such a production, Roberts had already established the stakes of the show and familiarized readers with its creative team. She had already provided evidence for why audiences needed to throw their support behind this trans-centric undertaking.

In addition to her many entries on Mock's transgender advocacy, as well as prior mentions of *Pose*'s Our Lady J, MJ Rodriguez, and Dominique Jackson, Roberts had followed cast member Angelica Ross since the start of her career. Ross appeared in *TransGriot* as early as 2007, when she shared a YouTube video about the need for more out and visible African American trans women (Roberts 2007a). In 2009, with the launch of Ross's album (available on Napster!), Roberts (2009) asked readers to "get [Ross's] career jump started." Readers can follow Ross's stratospheric rise in the subsequent decade, from the start of her blog and podcast (both of which have guest appearances by Roberts) to the founding of her tech company, TransTech Social Enterprises. By the time Roberts prompted readers about the importance of watching and supporting trans-driven television, she had laid a decade of groundwork, following the innovations of trans creatives and positioning *Pose* as a potential "springboard" for even more trans artists (Roberts 2018a).

Always with an eye for the structural, Roberts framed her support of *Pose* as one shaped by the long view of trans politics. She tells readers it is "imperative" that they support shows like *Pose* not just because it is well written and acted but also because the show's success could persuade more studios "to take a chance on producing more trans themed TV shows with trans actors in them, along with trans people writing the scripts" (Roberts 2018a). More trans-driven media, as Roberts has argued throughout the years, could not only channel resources and jobs to the trans community but also precipitate the cultural shifts required for legislative and other institutional changes. In her words, "In order for us to make progress on the trans civil rights front from a legislative and legal level, we also have to make progress in terms of how our images are portrayed in popular culture" (Roberts 2011a). In a media landscape bereft of opportunities for trans creatives, the success of a show like *Pose* could potentially "pave the way" for many others—but only if the trans community is able to regard their fates as interlinked.

As a veteran trans activist, Roberts was of course aware of limitations to mainstream media, electoral politics, and a legal system designed to criminalize Black transgender people. She often recounted the histories of abuse that US governmental and social institutions have inflicted on Black people and particularly Black trans people. She knew that, even when trans actors are "in the building," they have to "fight tooth and nail" for a modicum of recognition and respect (Roberts 2020). Paraphrasing Gil Scott Heron, she wrote, "The Black trans revolution will not be televised," noting that the most transformative changes will require intracommunity discussions and collective power built from intimate spaces (Roberts 2010). Still, Roberts also resisted dichotomizing arguments that presumed activists must either work as external agitators or become complicit assimilationists. Rather, she insisted on a t4t praxis that could connect revolutionary visioning with the necessary work of getting one another through the day-to-day. For Roberts, this meant supporting trans kin who could pressure prominent institutions from within while she wrote toward and built alternatives to those institutions.

Addressing recent enthusiasm for direction action protests, Roberts repeatedly emphasized the range of tactics involved in systemic transformation—as well as the diversity of people who can and should contribute differently to that change. In her early criticisms of Occupy Wall Street, Roberts (2011b) celebrated the power of direct action while also cautioning that "you need all the tools in the civil rights toolbox to enact systemic change." Months later, she followed up with a longer overview of the civil rights movement, discussing how marches and protests participated in a "long term strategy" that also involved lawsuits, voting rights expansions, and negotiations "with congressional and executive branch leaders to pass the legislative relief that African-Americans needed" (Roberts 2012b). In other words, Roberts's t4t care is guided by the potential of collective world making while also attending to immediate measures that will keep people alive. T4t love-politics is both a strategy for long-term transformation and a means of "getting by in the interregnum"—which, to return to the words of Malatino (2019: 657), "may end up being the only time we have." Especially within the "economies of scarcity" that Malatino describes as surrounding trans experience, love-politics fosters urgently needed mutual care through a commitment to proximity. We aspire to love, but even if we fall short, we commit to the collisions and collusions of our lives, and to the explorations of futures that can enable our collective thriving.

Living Together in the Only Time We Have

In October 2020 Roberts died from a pulmonary embolism. By November's Transgender Day of Remembrance (TDoR), she was still on many people's minds. As trans people and allies gathered to mark one of the most violent years in recent memory, many noted the somberness of doing so with this recent loss (Elahi 2020; Petoia and Vaz 2020; Rudolph 2020). Roberts had given many transgender people the language and space for mourning. In the sleepless hours after TDoR, her friend and partner in activism, Dee Dee Watters, shared her 4:00 a.m. reflections via Facebook. Watters (2020) recalled the two decades she had spent working alongside Roberts, fighting for respect and justice for trans victims. The two of them had driven between morgues and funeral homes. They met with victims' families, holding space for this raw grief while ensuring that trans people's stories were told with care. Queer journalist Dana Rudolph (2020) captures the legacy of this work in her own TDoR post—how Roberts not only combatted the injustice of these deaths but also demonstrated that there is "a story and a loss behind each and every one of the names on the memorial list." Though *TransGriot* garnered public attention for its coverage of trans murders, that coverage was especially remarkable for its emphasis on trans life.

Roberts deftly interwove stories of pain and loss into a t4t praxis oriented toward protecting trans lives and futures. She crowdsourced the trans community for photos and stories to counter the mugshots broadcast by mainstream media, challenging journalistic norms as she did so. She captured trans victims as "who they were to [the trans] community" (Watters 2020) and narrativized the impact of antitrans violence on the ones they left behind. "Your death wasn't in vain," she wrote to Gwen Araujo on the fifteenth anniversary of the teen's brutal murder. Tracing the legislative aftermath of Araujo's case, Roberts (2017b) drew a direct line between the Gwen Araujo Justice for Victims Act to California's eventual ban on trans and gay panic defenses. Likewise, on the anniversary of Brandon Teena's death, she chronicled how his murder "galvanized the trans community to action," catalyzing her own involvement in trans activism (Roberts 2013a). Though Teena was robbed of the time to fully explore his own identity, Roberts situates his experiences within a constellation of gender variance, and stories his legacy into an ongoing struggle against cisnormativity.

In her emphasis on resonant experiences—experiences that do not align perfectly with hers but instead "slant rhyme" with her encounters with race and/or gender (Malatino 2020: 54)—Roberts often reflected on the thin veil of luck that kept her and other trans folks off the list of names read on TDoR. In 2017, when Brenda Bostick was killed in New York, Roberts (2017c) wrote, "It could have been me." At age fifty-nine, Bostick was only four years older than Roberts, who was celebrating her fifty-fifth birthday on the day of Bostick's murder. Between their ages and their shared identities, Roberts found herself dwelling with this particular attack. Rather than individualizing this incident, however, Roberts turned again to the many ongoing conditions that direct violence toward Black trans women. Mobilizing her own relations, she addressed Black organizations and movements, emphasizing what folks should be doing now to protect their trans relations and kin.

Building on renewed public attention to racial injustice, Roberts challenged prominent Black organizations to consider the needs of transgender people within their own communities. She pointed to the absence of trans folks from the majority of campaigns, asking, "Why aren't you as loud and vocal about the murders of Black trans people as you have been for the Jordan Edwardses, Trayvon Martins, and Mike Browns of the world?" (Roberts 2017c). In her post, Roberts (2017c) addresses the NAACP, the Congressional Black Caucus, Black churches, and Black Lives Matter, asking them to "consistently back up those spoken words [*Black lives matter*]" by "prov[ing] you love and support your trans siblings." Again, Roberts's criticisms are not distant attacks from an outsider but, rather, an insistence that her relations acknowledge and value the Black trans women in their communities. She calls in "Black Lives Matter and other orgs working to uplift *our* people," reminding cisgender Black people that Black trans women are "your siblings" (Roberts 2017c; emphasis added). More, Black trans women have already been "doing our part to uplift all the communities we intersect and interact with" (Roberts 2017d). Black trans women have already extended their vulnerability, already embraced the proximity of their needs and futures with their cisgender kin, but they are continually denied reciprocal care.

Like other articulations of t4t, Roberts's t4t praxis responds to this "vacuum of care" left by the widespread abandonment of trans people (Malatino 2020: 70). Rather than pursuing trans separatism, though, Roberts's love-politics constellates trans experiences within broader networks of social relations. Especially given the many imbrications of antitrans and anti-Black violence, Roberts refused to sequester "trans issues" as if they were self-containing or isolatable from broader mechanisms of state and social harm. For her, for many Black trans people, and for trans people of color more broadly, such divisions are often not neat or even possible. The t4t world making that emerges from her writing, then, provides a "pattern of care and witness" (70) for her trans siblings and calls on other communities to see themselves as implicated in that social fabric. Roberts's t4t love-politics not only commits to urgent and necessary solidarities that sustain trans lives in the here and now but also extends that vulnerability to others whose lives intersect with the myriad trajectories of trans lives. This is not an assertion that "everyone is trans" but, rather, that everyone's lives affect and are affected by trans people and the conditions that attenuate trans lives.

In the origin story of t4t, the acronym names a refuge from trans-exclusionary dating spaces. If we trace this practice of proximity and mutual protection to a longer history of trans world making, however, we see how t4t prioritizes trans kinship and lives while also honoring trans people's embeddedness in other social and political communities. More, this t4t praxis creates the conditions for witnessing oft-occluded perspectives within all our communities. Roberts's love-politics finds connection through "a radical embrace of difference," positing trans folks and our many intersecting communities as "subjects who work on/against themselves to work for each other" (Nash 2013: 18). Through this practice, we can "dream of a yet unwritten future" (18) while securing enough resources and protections for trans people to do that dreaming.

When she first introduced her blog, Roberts wrote, "It is said that when a Griot dies, a library has burned to the ground." Undeniably, Trans World is poorer without Monica Roberts—a sister and mentor, a trove of trans wisdom, and a beacon of justice. With *TransGriot*, however, she gifted us a rich archive of resources for caring for one another in a world so intent on our destruction. In early 2021, in fact, Watters launched TransGriot, LLC, to continue Roberts's tireless documentation of trans history and innovation (Clifton 2021). Roberts taught us to write of and write toward trans abundance while capturing our losses. Her t4t praxis offers a politics through which our intimate connections become a driving force of systemic change. More, she mobilized t4t care toward a more just world while embracing the fact that care itself is a fraught, imperfect, and ongoing process. *TransGriot* thus envisions and aspires to radically inclusive love while grounding itself in the hard day-to-day work of sustaining our relationships and ourselves.

V. Jo Hsu is an assistant professor of rhetoric and writing at the University of Texas at Austin, where they are also core faculty in the Center for Asian American Studies and a faculty affiliate of the LGBTQ Studies Program. Jo's research interweaves gender studies, disability studies, and critical race studies to examine the interrelations of these social categories. They are interested in how expectations around racialized, gendered bodily norms affect the life chances and opportunities of those excluded by those very narratives. Their work can be found in disciplinary journals such as the *Quarterly Journal of Speech, Women's Studies in Communication*, and *College Composition and Communication*. Their creative writing has been nominated for a Pushcart Prize, and can be found in *Kartika Review, Color Bloq,* and other literary outlets. Throughout their (often wayward and meandering) academic journey, Jo has been fortunate to have the support of generous mentors and coconspirators, and they strive to further these forms of mutual care and collaborative worldbuilding.

Notes

1.   I follow Roberts's acronym here, highlighting those historically occluded within LGBTQ communities.
2.   Catherine Knight Steele's *Digital Black Feminism* (2021) also positions Roberts in a legacy of Black feminist technoculture, pointing to Black feminists' use of digital spaces to challenge gender binaries.

References

Ajani, Ashia. 2020. "How Monica Roberts Became One of America's Most Respected Black Trans Journalists." *Them*, February 29. www.them.us/story/monica-roberts-transgriot-profile.

Birnbaum, Emily. 2018. "LGBTQ Journalism Group Apologizes after Host Refers to Attendees at Event as 'Things and Its.'" *The Hill*, September 9. thehill.com/media/405797-lgbtq-journalism-group-apologizes-after-host-refers-to-attendees-at-event-as-things-and.

Chaudhry, V Varun. 2019. "Trans/Coalitional Love-Politics." *TSQ* 6, no. 4: 521–38. https://doi.org/10.1215/23289252-7771681.

Clifton, Derrick. 2021. "This Black, Trans Publication Will Honor Trailblazing Journalist Monica Roberts' Legacy." *Them*, January 13. www.them.us/story/transgriot-black-trans-publication-honors-monica-roberts-legacy.

Duque, Andres. 2008. "Transgender Latina Teen Murdered in Colorado." *Blabbeando* (blog), July 23. blabbeando.blogspot.com/2008/07/transgender-latina-teen-murdered-in.html.

Elahi, Amina. 2020. "Virtual Service Saturday for Transgender Day of Remembrance." WKMS, Murray State University, November 20. www.wkms.org/post/virtual-service-saturday-transgender-day-remembrance.

Ellison, Treva, Kai M. Green, Matt Richardson, and C. Riley Snorton. 2017. "We Got Issues: Toward a Black Trans*/Studies." *TSQ* 4, no. 2: 162–69. https://doi.org/10.1215/23289252 -3814949.

Friess, Steve. 2018. "Everybody's Wrong in NLGJA Fiasco." *Bay Area Reporter*, September 12. www .ebar.com/news/news//265307.

Green, Kai M., and Marquis Bey. 2017. "Where Black Feminist Thought and Trans* Feminism Meet: A Conversation." *Souls* 19, no. 4: 438–54.

Krell, Elías Cosenza. 2017. "Is Transmisogyny Killing Trans Women of Color? Black Trans Feminisms and the Exigencies of White Femininity." *TSQ* 4, no. 2: 226–42. https://doi.org /10.1215/23289252-3815033.

Kurutz, Steven. 2020. "Monica Roberts, Transgender Advocate and Journalist, Dies at Fifty-Eight." *New York Times*, October 13. www.nytimes.com/2020/10/13/us/monica-roberts-dead.html.

Malatino, Hil. 2019. "Future Fatigue: Trans Intimacies and Trans Presents (or How to Survive the Interregnum)." *TSQ* 6, no. 4: 635–58. https://doi.org/10.1215/23289252-7771796.

Malatino, Hil. 2020. *Trans Care*. Minneapolis: University of Minnesota Press.

Mock, Janet. 2020. "A Celebration of a Life of Activism and Education." *TransGriot* (blog). transgriot.com/about/.

Mukasa, Juliet Victor. 2006. "On Transgender Human Rights Issues in Africa." *TransGriot* (blog), December 22. transgriot.blogspot.com/2006/12/on-transgender-human-rights-issues-in .html.

Nash, Jennifer C. 2013. "Practicing Love: Black Feminism, Love-Politics, and Post-intersectionality." *Meridians* 11, no. 2: 1–24. https://doi.org/10.2979/meridians.11.2.1.

Nash, Jennifer C. 2019. *Black Feminism Reimagined: After Intersectionality*. Durham, NC: Duke University Press.

Petoia, Cabot, and Shai Vaz. 2020. "National Black Justice Coalition Statement on Transgender Day of Remembrance." National Black Justice Coalition, November 19. nbjc.org/media -center/releases/nbjc-statement-on-transgender-day-remembrance.

Roberts, Latoya. 2020. "A Celebration of Love for the Life of Monica Roberts." Texas Obituary Project. www.texasobituaryproject.org/2020/10/Monica/Monica%20Program.pdf.

Roberts, Monica. 2006a. "A Black 'Transamerica.'" *TransGriot* (blog), April 1. transgriot.blogspot .com/2006/04/black-transamerica.html.

Roberts, Monica. 2006b. "Transgender Teen Shut Out of Prom." *TransGriot* (blog), May 25. transgriot.blogspot.com/2006/05/transgender-teen-shut-out-of-prom.html.

Roberts, Monica. 2006c. "What's a Griot?" *TransGriot* (blog), January 5. transgriot.blogspot.com /2006/01/whats-griot.html.

Roberts, Monica. 2007a. "Angelica's Had It Up to Here (And So Have I)." *TransGriot* (blog), February 12. transgriot.blogspot.com/2007/02/angelicas-had-it-up-to-here.html.

Roberts, Monica. 2007b. "Black Transgender TV Characters." *TransGriot* (blog), February 23. transgriot.blogspot.com/2007/02/black-transgender-tv-characters.html.

Roberts, Monica. 2007c. "Can't Y'all Read Your Own Stylebooks?" *TransGriot* (blog), September 8, 2007. transgriot.com/cant-yall-read-your-own-stylebooks/.

Roberts, Monica. 2007d. "The Color Line IS a Transgender Community Problem Too." *TransGriot* (blog), July 16. transgriot.blogspot.com/2007/07/color-line-is-transgender-community .html.

Roberts, Monica. 2008a. "Another Transwoman Murdered, Another Media Diss." *TransGriot* (blog), July 22. transgriot.blogspot.com/2008/07/another-transwoman-murdered-another.html.

Roberts, Monica. 2008b. "Are Black Transwomen Fighting a Lost Cause?" *TransGriot* (blog), August 13. transgriot.blogspot.com/2008/08/are-black-transwomen-fighting-lost.html.

Roberts, Monica. 2008c. "Family of Murdered Transwoman Seeks Justice." *TransGriot* (blog), July 6. transgriot.blogspot.com/2008/07/family-of-murdered-transwoman-seeks.html.

Roberts, Monica. 2008d. "I Repeat: Can't Y'all Read Your Own Stylebooks?" *TransGriot* (blog), May 16, 2008. transgriot.blogspot.com/2008/05/i-repeat-cant-yall-read-your-own.html.

Roberts, Monica. 2008e. "I Went Off . . . Got Quoted . . . and Got Results." *TransGriot* (blog), July 27. transgriot.blogspot.com/2008/07/i-went-offgot-quotedand-got-results.html.

Roberts, Monica. 2008f. "Why Black Transgender Issues Are Black Community Issues." *TransGriot* (blog), July 25. transgriot.blogspot.com/2008/07/why-black-transgender-issues-are-black.html.

Roberts, Monica. 2009. "'Spotlight' on Angelica Ross." *TransGriot* (blog), February 8. transgriot.blogspot.com/2009/02/spotlight-on-angelica-ross.html.

Roberts, Monica. 2010. "The Black Trans Revolution Will Not Be Televised." *TransGriot* (blog), October 4. transgriot.blogspot.com/2010/10/black-trans-revolution-will-not-be.html.

Roberts, Monica. 2011a. "Hollywood Is as Important to Trans People as Washington DC." *TransGriot* (blog), March 22. transgriot.blogspot.com/2011/03/hollywood-is-as-important-to-trans.html.

Roberts, Monica. 2011b. "Occupy Wall Street Needs to Occupy the Voting Booths as Well." *TransGriot* (blog), October 18. transgriot.blogspot.com/2011/10/occupy-wall-street-needs-to-occupy.html.

Roberts, Monica. 2011c. "Shaping the New Black Trans Paradigm." *TransGriot* (blog), November 1. transgriot.blogspot.com/2011/11/shaping-new-black-trans-paradigm.html.

Roberts, Monica. 2012a. "Black Community, It's Past Time to Fight for Black Trans Women's Human Rights." *TransGriot* (blog), June 12. transgriot.blogspot.com/2012/06/black-community-its-past-time-to-fight.html.

Roberts, Monica. 2012b. "Direct Action Protests Alone Don't Get You Human Rights Coverage." *TransGriot* (blog), April 25. transgriot.blogspot.com/2012/04/direct-action-protests-alone-dont-get.html.

Roberts, Monica. 2012c. "Mia Nikasimo: Transgender Community as an African in the Diaspora." *TransGriot* (blog), November 1. transgriot.blogspot.com/2012/11/mia-nikasimo-transgender-community-as.html.

Roberts, Monica. 2012d. "Why Black Gay and Trans Americans Need More than Marriage Equality Report." *TransGriot* (blog), January 20. transgriot.blogspot.com/2012/01/why-black-gay-and-trans-americans-need.html.

Roberts, Monica. 2013a. "Brandon Teena Murder Twentieth Anniversary." *TransGriot* (blog), December 31. transgriot.blogspot.com/2013/12/brandon-teena-murder-20th-anniversary.html.

Roberts, Monica. 2013b. "Colorism Needs to Cease and Desist in the Black Trans Community." *TransGriot* (blog), August 13. transgriot.blogspot.com/2013/08/colorism-needs-to-cease-and-desist-in.html.

Roberts, Monica. 2013c. "Race and Class Still Matter in the Trans Community." *TransGriot* (blog), May 7. transgriot.blogspot.com/2013/05/race-and-class-still-matter-in-trans.html.

Roberts, Monica. 2014. "Creating Change 2014—Day 3 Recap." *TransGriot* (blog), February 1. transgriot.blogspot.com/2014/02/creating-change-2014-day-3-recap.html.

Roberts, Monica. 2015. "Andrea Jenkins Gets Added to the Congressional Record!" *TransGriot* (blog), May 22. transgriot.blogspot.com/2015/05/andrea-jenkins-gets-added-to.html.

Roberts, Monica. 2016a. "Andrea's Running for Minneapolis City Council!" *TransGriot* (blog), December 20. transgriot.blogspot.com/2016/12/andreas-running-for-minneapolis-city.html.

Roberts, Monica. 2016b. "Hey Hollywood, Trans Actors Exist, So Hire Them!" *TransGriot* (blog) September 12. transgriot.blogspot.com/2016/09/hey-hollywood-trans-actors-exist-so.html.

Roberts, Monica. 2017a. "Can You Donate and Help Trans Candidates Make History?" *TransGriot* (blog), November 1. transgriot.blogspot.com/2017/11/can-you-donate-and-help-trans .html.

Roberts, Monica. 2017b. "Gwen Araujo Murder Fifteenth Anniversary." *TransGriot* (blog), October 4. transgriot.blogspot.com/2017/10/gwen-araujo-murder-15th-anniversary.html.

Roberts, Monica. 2017c. "My Thoughts about Brenda Bostick's Murder." *TransGriot* (blog), May 8. transgriot.blogspot.com/2017/05/my-thoughts-about-brenda-bosticks-murder.html.

Roberts, Monica. 2017d. "TransGriot: We Black Trans Women Stand Up for Everyone—When Will People Stand Up for Us?" *TransGriot* (blog), February 27. transgriot.blogspot.com /2017/02/we-black-trans-women-stand-up-for.html.

Roberts, Monica. 2017e. "Trans United Fund Deserves Your Support." *TransGriot* (blog), November 29. transgriot.blogspot.com/2017/11/trans-united-fund-deserves-your-support.html.

Roberts, Monica. 2018a. "If You Want Trans TV Shows, Gotta Watch Them." *TransGriot* (blog), July 5. transgriot.blogspot.com/2018/07/if-you-want-trans-tv-shows-gotta-watch.html.

Roberts, Monica. 2018b. "Moni's Thoughts about the 2018 NLGJA Convention Closing Reception." *TransGriot* (blog), September 10. transgriot.blogspot.com/2018/09/monis-thoughts-about -2018-nlgja.html.

Roberts, Monica. 2018c. "Moni's Thoughts on the Friess Op-Ed." *TransGriot* (blog), September 13. transgriot.blogspot.com/2018/09/monis-thoughts-on-friess-op-ed.html.

Roberts, Monica. 2018d. "Trans World, Stop Bashing Trans Sex Workers!" *TransGriot* (blog), April 8. transgriot.blogspot.com/2018/04/trans-world-stop-bashing-trans-sex.html.

Roberts, Monica. 2020. "Trans Actors Can Be in the Building and Still Get Ignored." *TransGriot* (blog), July 31. transgriot.blogspot.com/2020/07/trans-actors-can-be-in-building-and .html.

Rudolph, Dana. 2020. "Transgender Day of Remembrance 2020." *Mombian* (blog), November 20. mombian.com/2020/11/20/transgender-day-of-remembrance-2020/.

Snorton, C. Riley. 2017. *Black on Both Sides: A Racial History of Trans Identity*. Minneapolis: University of Minnesota Press.

Spillers, Hortense J. 1987. "Mama's Baby, Papa's Maybe: An American Grammar Book." *Diacritics* 17, no. 2: 64–81. https://doi.org/10.2307/464747.

Steele, Catherine Knight. 2021. *Digital Black Feminism*. New York: New York University Press.

Watters, DeeDee. 2020. "Long Post Can't Go Back to Sleep." *Facebook*, November 21. www .facebook.com/theofficialdeedee/posts/3569363746419490.

WMC Action News 5. 2008. "Police Explore Motives in Shooting Death of Transgendered Prosti- tute." July 3. www.wmcactionnews5.com/story/8615577/police-explore-motives-in-shooting -death-of-transgendered-prostitute.

Transtocar, Three Fragments

CYNTHIA CITLALLIN DELGADO HUITRÓN

1. In a Footnote

This essay began in a footnote—number 2—located at the end of a sentence in the penultimate paragraph of the first section of my article "Haptic Tactic: Hyper-tenderness of the [Mexican] State and the Performances of Lia García," published in this very journal (Delgado Huitrón 2019: 167). The article approaches the hypertender touch of transfeminist artist, poet, and pedagogue Lia García (La Novia Sirena) through a close analysis of a performance event entitled "Quinceañera," part of her larger performative project *Proyecto 10Bis* (2016–17). In the article I propose using the anglophone composite *to transgender touch* for thinking about what trans embodiment does to the transitivity of touch. A grammatically incorrect (and perhaps controversial) formulation that makes of *transgender* a verb, *to transgender touch* intends to foreground the performative force that trans touch holds, in its capacity to *do* and its ability to *un*do, notions of gender and sexuality as abided and prescribed by the law. The sentence where this footnote is located introduces the term and inserts, between em dashes and in italics, the Spanish-language word *transtocar*. Instead of doing the explanatory work of translation, however, the footnote takes the reader to the crevices of the article only to offer up another creative, grammatically incorrect formulation that defers and disrupts meaning once more. The footnote explains that *transtocar* is the alteration of the Spanish-language word *trastocar* by way of an *n* in its midst: *trastocar* becomes "transtocar." Withholding a "definitive" translation, the footnote offers a different linguistic (and therefore cultural) referent and then enacts the same creative and grammatically disruptive act onto language as that which conceives of *to transgender touch*: it alters the order established by its semantic construction.

At once serious and playful, much of the work of translation happens in footnotes. Footnotes are the space in which original text or text in translation is inserted, engaging in direct translation and sometimes incorporating the possible different inflections and cultural connotations that these words might have. This form of bilingual academic writing serves to justify word choice and also to provide ease to the (assumed anglophone) reader in their journey through the text. Annotations, sidenotes, disclaimers, afterthoughts—the footnote is on the order of the fragment. Part of the main text but seemingly standing on its own, these pieces of writing hold thinking that gets easily tossed aside. Footnotes are also the location of the common authorial declaration, "translation mine." In this particular footnote, however, I do not set out to provide or claim an authoritative translation. Instead, I explain that these two lexical formulations, *to transgender touch* and *transtocar*, are conceived alongside each other, much in the spirit of queer and performance theorist Eve Kosofky Sedgwick's (2003: 8–9) *beside*. In contrast to the logic and authority of the translative footnote, the footnote that concerns this essay performs a disruption to the power relations embedded within the translative footnote as genre by exposing the very act of thinking and theorizing across languages.

Perhaps I succumbed too quickly to the allure of the *beside*, its spatial arrangement and its connotation of accompaniment, when in reality thinking trans-lingually engages the much messier spatiality of the overlap, the montage, something approximating Gloria Anzaldúa's *nepantla*. When crossed by geographic and linguistic borders, thinking and feeling, and therefore theorizing, entail a natural flow between one's languages at the psychic and embodied levels of the self. It is an unconscious operation that does not require us to code switch, releasing the heaviness of the tongue and its supposed illegitimacy. A tongue, Anzaldúa (2012: 81) suggests, that must be left to move wildly.

There is always trouble in the wildness of translation. There is the trouble of loss: the loss of exactitude or of referential completeness premised on a fear of the irretrievability of what falls into the cracks of cultural translation. There is the trouble of loyalty: to the text, to the original and to origin; of betrayal, of misrepresenting or misunderstanding, premised on the fear of facing the truth of difference, the false promise of mimesis. There is the trouble of the political: of epistemic impositions, of unidirectional prescriptions, of power imbalances, of knowing that words and concepts are sites of struggle. And there is the problem of translation par excellence: having to navigate between a calculated loyalty to meaning and a felt commitment to poetic style. All these concerns cause trouble, time and time again, and are thus tackled, in praxis, through constant experimentation: by mixing languages (Spanglish, Portuñol), by refusing to translate words (*travesti*, *lencha*), by resignification (*queer* to *cuir* to *kuir*).

While all this trouble haunts my footnote, this moment of translation emerged from another, more quiet concern, *una inquietud*. It was not the transfer of meaning from one language to another that unsettled me (although it was that too). What disquieted me was transcribing into English a form of touch that I had felt and experienced in another language. Does touch, as a sensorial language, also happen through spoken and written tongues? Do movement and gesture, sense and sensation, translate? And if so, what are the textures of such translations?

2. Transtocar

A disruption to *trastocar*, *transtocar* wears the mark of what it intends: to semantically alter or perturb both gender and touch. In the *Diccionario panhispánico de dudas*, published by Real Academia Española (RAE)—an institution I cite with great ambivalence—the verb *trastocar*, formed by the prefix *tras-* followed by the verb *tocar*, is defined as 1) *trastornar o alterar algo*, and in a reflexive form as 2) *trastornarse o perturbarse.*[1] Broadly, then, *trastocar* means to alter or change something, with the unsettling yet at times desirable inflection of an action that is upsetting, perturbing, disrupting, or subverting.

That the verb *tocar* is transitive already establishes a subject/object relation premised on an action. It involves a movement and therefore a transition between or across two or more entities: *tocar*, to touch another; *ser tocado*, to be touched by another; or *tocarse*, to touch oneself. In this way *tocar* is already *trastocar*, *to touch* is already *to touch across, to touch through, to trans-touch*. This speaks to the way that *touch*, *tocar*, and even *toucher* in French are used to express a change or alteration. Think here of Ben Sifuentes-Jáuregui's (2002: 2) proposed triad of a touch that alters at the level of discourse: *On a touché au vers* (from Stéphane Mallarmé), *on a touché à la critique* (from Paul de Man), and his additional third term, *on a touché le genre*, as it emerges from "the transvestite['s] whispering: 'He trastocado el género.'" It is this last formulation, in the textures of a whisper, with which *transtocar* converses.[2]

The disordering the *n* provokes is semantic, political, and aesthetic. The semantic disruption occurs at the level of the word. The prefix *tras-* in *trastocar* is a simplified version of the prefix *trans-*, and it is nearly interchangeable with it. However, according to Spanish grammar rules, the *n* is removed when the prefix is used to denote a place situated *detrás* or behind the space designated by the base word.[3] I bring up this onerous detail because it both emphasizes the spatiality of the prefix and elucidates the degree to which the addition of the *n* is a mischievous endeavor. Adding the *n* in italics is to resist convention as well as to alter the word *trastocar* itself. This way *transtocar* enters a contemporary (and playful) vernacular that makes explicit reference to a gender, sexual identity, and embodiment that the *RAE* disavows. With the outright rejection of any alteration to language that experiments with more gender inclusive expressions, as, for example, the use of the letters *e* and *x* to replace the gendered *o* for its plural forms, the institution forecloses language's alterability, and with it its translatability. This is part of the political disruption of the *n*.

But this political disruption is also at the level of meaning. Returning to the *RAE*'s definition of *trastocar*, we gather the first word used to define it is "trastornar." This word conjures up a range of medical and specifically pathological connotations, especially its noun form, *trastorno*.[4] Used in a similar way as *disorder* in English, it is the language of mental and pyschological diagnosis: *un trastorno mental*, a mental disorder. For this reason, the vernacular use of *trastornar* tends toward an injurious use, referring to being or going "crazy." In fact, gender dysphoria was previously known as "trastorno de identidad de género."[5] This pathological inflection is embedded in the meaning of *trastocar*, also as a capacity to dis-order. The insertion of the *n* in *transtocar*, then, also serves to push back against this use and instead works toward a resignification of its pathological textures, especially with regard to gender and sexuality.

Finally, *transtocar* is also an aesthetic disruption. The *n* is unapologetically ornamental. It is the accent piece in the word's wardrobe—the accessory that always risks being too much, in excess, edging kitsch. It disturbs, it disrupts, it dis-orders, just enough to make a statement that ripples in the hegemony of language.

There is much to be said about what happens in the space between the Spanish *transtocar* and the English *to transgender touch*. In lieu of the skillful travestismo between verb, noun, and adjective that *to transgender touch* enacts, we have the playful *travesura* of the interruption of the *n* in *transtocar*, a one-word verb easy on the Latinate tongue. It is clear by now that in the fortresses of grammar, as in those of gender, both reassemblings are technically incorrect. There is something of the vulnerable in both words and in the gap between them—so present yet forced into hiding by the virtue of translation. And while something might appear to get lost in the space between *transgender touch* and *transtocar*, having been conceived simultaneously evinces this loss to be a dialogical transaction instead, a form of thinking developed already in and as translation. Such creative disposition follows Walter Benjamin's (2015) understanding of translation as a mode whereby the act of translating must focus on translating a language's mode of signification, rather than merely its meaning. That is, not just the object each word intends (to signify) but also the space in which it comes to intend such a thing. In other words, the infrastructure of language, and not just of each word, must be made palpable in translation. For this reason, it is not that something gets lost in the gap between one and the other, between *transtocar* and *to transgender touch*, but that each contains fragments of the other. To conceive of something in translation, then, forcibly means to translate one's own tender disposition, to acknowledge one's own split tongue and psyche—one's own fragments.

3. Fragments of a Vessel

Lia García collects broken dishes. This impulse emerged from a performance she called "Cocinar la Memoria" (2018), performed during an artist residency at the living museum Elsewhere, in Greensboro, North Carolina. Once a secondhand shop owned and run by Sylvia Gray, this three-story building downtown contains a vast array of old objects, from furniture to clothing to artworks. The premise of the residency was to use any and as many of the archived objects as desired and make with/of them a new artistic object or intervention. Surrounded by sculptors, García felt slightly out of place; the medium seemed to present some translative trouble of its own.[6]

"Cooking Memory" consisted of moving three boxes from the space of the attic to the space of the kitchen with the help of a participatory audience. These boxes, each of which she labeled differently—*Justicia, Fragilidad, Sueños*—were full of broken dishes, *pedacitos de vidrio y porcelana*. Putting these *trastes rotos* on a table, García declared this to be the return of the dishes to their "rightful" place, an act of justice, dreaming, and fragility. With the dishes no longer relegated to the attic, García enabled their leaping movement of "return" to what she considered to be their original, and therefore rightful, place. García, however, does not merely consider this a return to an origin, "*a su raíz*" in her words, but an act of rescue, *rescatándoles del olvido*. This movement made the dishes travel from a relegated space that deemed them useless to the rife space of memory: "Tal vez esos trastes nunca imaginaron que alguien los iba a rescatar y los iba a hacer transitar de lo inservible a la memoria."[7] Thinking the kitchen as the dishes' original place is enacting a mode of signification that follows a specific spatial and taxonomic distribution: that dishes belong in a kitchen or on a dining-room table. In a way, García engages in a process of translation, attempting to speak the broken dishes' language and then transferring that meaning to her own performance. The kitchen may have been, in García's view, the dishes' place of origin, yet the dishes are certainly not in their original form but in disassembled fragments of themselves, shuffled and dis-ordered into heaping boxes of shards.

In this performance, García writes and conducts a score for translation. The choreographed movement from attic to kitchen, arguably not one of translation in the strict sense, nods to the form of the movement between a translation and its original. There is a reciprocal relationship between these two spaces, just as there is between languages, and expressing such relation, Benjamin (2015: 73) argues, is the purpose of translation. Translation, as a manifestation of the kinship of languages, must not strive for likeness with the original, "for in its afterlife— which could not be called that if it were not a transformation and renewal of something living—the original undergoes a change" (73). In "Cooking Memory," neither the movement of the dishes to the kitchen nor the dishes themselves strive for likeness to an imagined original location or original form. Instead, the performance foregrounds the transformation and changes that have occurred and that grant these broken pieces their afterlife, even if this is in the shape of memory.

The shards of these broken dishes, like words in language, are always already fragments of a whole. Of broken dishes and translation, Benjamin writes,

> Fragments of a vessel which are to be glued together must match one another in the smallest details, although they need not be like one another. In the same way a translation, instead of resembling the meaning of the original, must *lovingly and in detail* incorporate the original's mode of signification, thus making both the original and the translation recognizable as fragments of a greater language, just as fragments are part of a vessel. (79; emphasis mine)

While in "Cooking Memory" García does not engage in the task of gluing fragments of broken dishes back together, her broader movement, from attic to kitchen, incorporates the same mode of signification, its intended effect, through this performance of return and reassembly. The task of the translator thus lies in reassembling fragments "lovingly and in detail," where the original text and its translation, the original location and the movement of return, are recognized to be "fragments of a greater language," a process that requires a tender touch and a poetic closeness.

Thinking about the fragment makes us leap back to Anzaldúa (2012), who takes fragmentation—of the self, of consciousness, and of the body—to be a given, a kind of point of departure, even if in the midst of things. This fragmented state, which she calls the Coyolxauhqui state, is counteracted by its own impulse toward recomposition, "the psychic and creative process of tearing apart and pulling together," a deconstruction followed by reconstruction of a new order (50). In this dismemberment, re-membering is also an act of survival. And in the push-and-pull of fragmentation, in the kinship of languages, the small piece that alters *transtocar*—an *n*—shuffles meaning and re-members the word.

Translating, much like touching, requires a certain predisposition to being moved and in movement. A willingness not unlike the movement of broken dishes from the attic to the kitchen; or the reading of a footnote where your eyes must leap from the main text and into the crevices at the bottom of a page. Benjamin (2015: 81) writes, "Just as a tangent touches a circle lightly and at but one point . . . a translation touches the original lightly," and—as García might say, tenderly—"only at the infinitely small point of the sense, *thereupon pursuing its own course* according to the laws of fidelity in the freedom of linguistic flux" (emphasis mine). To pursue its own course, to follow its own impulse, is to free the fragment from its original order. To collect broken dishes, as Lia García does, is to archive the possibility of other orders and the potential of a different future recomposition and re-membering. It is to follow the thrust of *transtocar*.

Cynthia Citlallin Delgado Huitrón is a dissertation fellow and PhD candidate in performance studies at New York University. Her dissertation, "Staging the Interstice," theorizes the relationship between urban space and trans- embodiment by looking to performances that unfold in interstitial locations—such as the prison, the subway, the cabaret, and the rooftop. Her work has appeared, or is forthcoming, in *TSQ, Women and Performance, Hysteria Revista*, and *Gender, Place, and Culture*.

Notes

1. *Diccionario panhispánico de dudas*, s.v. "*trastocar*," www.rae.es/dpd/trastocar.
2. Parenthetically, *tocar* in Spanish also means "to play," as in to play an instrument, which tells us much about the inextricability of performance and the sensorial.
3. *Diccionario de la Real Academia Española*, s.v. "*tras-*," www.rae.es/dpd/tras-.
4. Thank you to Cole Rizki for emphasizing this in our conversations.
5. The latest version of the *Diagnostic and Statistical Manual of Mental Disorders*, the *DSM-5*, has removed this from its diagnostic categories; gender dysphoria remains.
6. Pers. comm., May 2021. Thank you, as always, to my dear friend Lia García, for the tender disposition to share her work and processes with me.
7. Memoria, here, reverberates in discourses and practices of public mourning specific to a context defined by the real violence of feminicides and disappearance.

References

Anzaldúa, Gloria. 2012. *Borderlands/La Frontera: The New Mestiza*. San Francisco: Aunt Lute.

Benjamin, Walter. 2015. "The Task of the Translator." In *Illuminations*, translated by Harry Zorn, 70–82. London: Bodley Head.

Delgado Huitrón, Cynthia Citlallin. 2019. "Haptic Tactic: Hyper-tenderness for the [Mexican] State and the Performances of Lia García." *TSQ* 6, no. 2: 164–79.

Sedgwick, Eve Kosofky. 2003. *Touching Feeling: Affect, Pedagogy, Performativity*. Durham, NC: Duke University Press.

Sifuentes-Jáuregui, Ben. 2002. *Travestism, Masculinity, and Latin American Literature*. New York: Palgrave.

Trans-Love, Cinematic Bodies, and Optical Desire Reimagined

ISAAC PREISS

Shimmering Images: Trans Cinema, Embodiment, and the Aesthetics of Change
Eliza Steinbock
Durham, NC: Duke University Press, 2019. 231 pp.

Experience has a way of resisting representation. When it emerges into the sphere of perceptibility, it does so as fleeting refraction. *Shimmering Images: Trans Cinema, Embodiment, and the Aesthetics of Change* investigates these moments of fugitive recognition, conceiving them as aesthetic, affective, and perceptual events or "shimmers." Eliza Steinbock intervenes in certain of transgender studies' inaugural queries around embodiment, textuality, and epistemology by attending to the many luminous concordances between transgender life and moving image media. *Shimmering Images* ventures to understand cinema and transness as engaged in a mutually poietic assemblage, producing effects and affects "through the bodily practice and technological principle of disjunction" (6).

Articulating this affinity anew, Steinbock is following a trajectory in transgender studies that seeks to complicate questions of visibility and representation, marked notably by the paradox introduced by Tourmaline, Eric A. Stanley, and Johanna Burton (2017: xv–xvi): increased "positive representation" can also indicate, for trans women of color especially, increased subjection to violence. Responding to this problematic, *Shimmering Images* takes a discursive detour away from the scene of "reveal," a ubiquitous filmic strategy that, subjecting trans bodies to violent or coerced exposure, posits transness as the limit case for visual knowing and, in doing so, continues to affirm the epistemological primacy of the optically determined real. *Shimmering Images* locates the violence of such moments not in the reveal itself but in a larger ontoepistemological logic "in which being

TSQ: Transgender Studies Quarterly ∗ Volume 9, Number 1 ∗ February 2022
DOI 10.1215/23289252-9475579 © 2022 Duke University Press

and knowing are always already entangled" (29). Steinbock's shimmer bypasses the reveal and illuminates alternative sites of meaning and magnitude outside representation per se, in variable processes of feeling, desiring, and becoming.

Steinbock's "inventory of shimmers" borrows from theories of or references to the word by Michel Foucault, Gilles Deleuze, Susan Stryker, and Steven Shaviro. Standing out as particularly influential is Roland Barthes (read in part through Gregory Seigworth and Melissa Gregg), whose shimmer is an affective mode of change or difference constituted "according to the angle of the subject's gaze" within an "integrally and almost exhaustively nuanced space" (10). It describes disjunction as it constitutes experience: how moments emerge from time spans, proximities from spaces, shades from gradients. Its articulation as such is also distinctly cinematic, recalling the film image as a flickering procession of still frames, which, through the spectator's optical, linguistic, and psychosocial capacities, take on the character of a dynamic whole. The shimmer thus offers a new framework through which to engage the affinities between cinema and transgender life grounded in the complex topographies of experience, as opposed to binary schematics of exposure/privacy, reveal/conceal, deception/truthfulness. If any knowable condition approaches, even asymptotically, what might be essentially "transgender," *Shimmering Images* suggests, it can be found in the always-close proximity of transgender life to what is changeable and affectable. Traces of that ephemeral referent are inscribed in the stories we tell and the media we produce (13).

The word *transgender*, of course, represents a heterogeneity of lives and experiences, and Steinbock, through a great deal of care and methodological rigor, demonstrates their commitment to using transness as an analytic device without giving way to reductive essentialization or metaphor. This omnipresent nuance, constitutive of actual populations, is achieved in part through the text's triadic structure—three conceptual models, each which evokes a cinematic/surgical practice and is indicated by an associated verb and typographic symbol: cut (/), suture (-), and multiply (*). Applying this dynamic organizing principle, Steinbock carefully distills from a variegated selection of media objects their obscure shimmerings, capturing scintillas of affect as they become momentarily unburdened from knowledge. What emerges in this process is a series of radical possibilities, especially regarding desire. In precinematic attractions (under the "cut" heading), this moment is found in the trick edit, a curious mechanism that delighted nineteenth-century publics, as it allowed them to "indulge in the spectacle of bodies doing weird and wonderful things, such as going to the moon or having a sex change" (40). Steinbock locates another shimmer mechanism in transmasculine docu-pornography (under "suture"), made over a century later, in which shimmering generates a cathectic counterlogic, rendering erotic those in its encounter through "darkness and other devalued affective modes of being" (93). A glistening reorientation occurs again in experimental works made at the turn of the twenty-first century (under "multiply"), whose non- or quasinarratives employ visual strategies of looping, patching, and distorting to effect something of desire unbounded from the human. In each instance of shimmering's splices, weaves, and multiplications, experience is evoked, as in Walter Benjamin's elusive *Erfahrung*, as something that occurs nonlocally, spanning spaces, communities, and histories.

Throughout *Shimmering Images*, the complex, multiply constitutive nature of Steinbock's subject (described aptly as "trans-inter-queer assemblage") is never neglected (20). As such, the text's discursive project is always in a dialectical engagement with its material stakes. Shimmering is a theoretical mechanism, but it always runs parallel to Steinbock's "trans-loving" praxis: "becom[ing] receptive to shimmers, or . . . seeing its more-than-stereo optics" (2, 10). Trans-loving functions (along with its twin disposition, cinephilia) in *Shimmering Images* as a call to action—urging readers to be generous in their love, to be patient with and open to the opacities of others as with themselves, and to do the deliberate and difficult work of producing knowledge and desire anew. Offering insight into how systemic cruelty is mediated by culturally determined epistemes, *Shimmering Images* provides a practical framework for how we can interface with these systems, as trans people and trans-lovers, in potentially resistant or subversive ways.

Isaac Preiss is a PhD student at the University of California, Berkeley, in the Department of Film and Media. His research is focused on cinematic mediations of transgender subjectivity and storytelling.

Reference

Tourmaline, Eric A. Stanley, and Johanna Burton. "Known Unknowns: An Introduction to Trap Door." *Trap Door: Trans Cultural Production and the Politics of Visibility*, edited by Tourmaline, Eric A. Stanley, and Johanna Burton, xv–xxvi. Cambridge, MA: MIT Press, 2017.

Trans in Retrospect
An Autotheory of Becoming

LAUREN FOURNIER

Reverse Cowgirl
McKenzie Wark
South Pasadena, CA: Semiotext(e), 2020. 200 pp.

Reverse Cowgirl describes itself as "an auto-ethnography of the opacity of the self." The book follows the renowned hacker/new media theorist and writer McKenzie Wark's reflecting on her trans identity; she does so through narrativizing her sex life and its relation to her gender identity via bold vignettes. She thoughtfully scans the landscape of her desires and identifications, historically and into the present, processing and theorizing her experiences as she goes. I would describe *Reverse Cowgirl* as an autotheory ("self" and "theory") in which Wark narrativizes her first-person lived experiences and engenders a personal theory of transness by reflecting on her life up to this point. The reader follows Wark through an understanding of her trans identity in retrospect, with Wark moving through autobiographical scenes in the 1980s, 1990s, and 2000s that were shaped by plea-sure, jouissance, and identity confusion—all told from a more confidently trans present. We come to see Wark where she is now, transitioning in her fifties, with her understanding both trans experience and her larger body of work through candid sharing. It is an absorptive, narrative style of writing in which theory hums below the surface—another drive, like sex. Engaging a nascent autotheoretical mode that is still in process, Wark seeks a language through which to articulate experiences that might have once been nameless or nebulous.

In a recent conversation about autotheory, Wark asks, "How can we be conceptual about the mundane?" (Fournier and Wark 2020). How can we engender theory and concepts from our particular lived experiences? This is a question at

TSQ: Transgender Studies Quarterly ★ Volume 9, Number 1 ★ February 2022   **129**
DOI 10.1215/23289252-9475593   © 2022 Duke University Press

the heart of the autotheoretical turn, and one of which Wark's *Reverse Cowgirl* provides one example. Autotheory has the potential for taking seriously the ethics and politics and aesthetics of one's own life—including, of course, one's sex life and gender identity. This is not new for the field of transgender studies, which, not unlike the fields of feminisms and women's and gender studies, has roots in autobiographically grounded academic and critical work—for example, the "personal criticism" Nancy K. Miller describes as characterizing much academic work in these emergent departments in the 1980s, which would set some of the groundwork for the eventual development of trans studies in the 1990s and the publication of formative works like Leslie Feinberg's arguably autofictional novel *Stone Butch Blues* (1993), Kate Bornstein's critical memoir *Gender Outlaw* (1994), and more recent works like Janet Mock's *Redefining Realness: My Path to Womanhood, Identity, Love, and So Much More* (2014), Juliet Jacques's *Trans* (2015), or Kai Cheng Thom's *Fierce Femmes and Notorious Liars: A Dangerous Trans Girl's Confabulous Memoir* (2019).

In seeking a language to articulate her trans identity, Wark also seeks to write in an embodied way—a tendency found in longer histories of feminist and queer writing and performance. Wark takes this drive toward "writing the body" to a humorous, logical conclusion when she includes a "user's manual" guide on "how to fuck this book." Her book on fucking, then, becomes something the reader can fuck, intimating that the reader can fuck Wark too, in a certain sense. The book, folded, can become a glory hole, a sock, or a papery orifice, like a cunt or an ass. In this way, Wark willfully and radically extends the erotics of reading—a theme that arises in other autotheoretical literature, including Maggie Nelson's *Argonauts* (notably and thoroughly problematized by many trans readers and scholars, who take issue with Nelson's appropriation of transgender experience when she places it alongside her cisgender experience of pregnancy and childbirth) or earlier autotheoretical works like Audre Lorde's *Uses of the Erotic* and Eve Kosofsky Sedgwick's *Touching Feeling*. With its explicit approach to erotics, *Reverse Cowgirl* is at home with autotheory and critical memoirs like Paul B. Preciado's *Testo Junkie* and Jeremy Atherton Lin's *Gay Bar: Why We Went Out*.

Like so much autotheoretical work, Wark's book is not just about herself but, fundamentally, herself as she exists in relation to others. I liked Wark's hailing of the citations at the end as a "chorus," positioning the range of intertexts with which she writes alongside as accompanying voices that narrativize and sing—polyphonic, melodic. There's something delightfully dramatic about it: the citations as akin to a chorus in a Greek tragedy that allows us to follow the action of the main plot (or line of argument). Only here it is our first-person narrator, Wark herself, writing her life in light of a coming-of-age as trans, and it doesn't read as a tragedy so much as a tragedy, plus time. While she is playful in the book, bringing a keen sense of humor to her deep self-awareness, she does not shirk the seriousness of her topics and does not hide the tragedies of lives lost to drug addiction—something she discusses anecdotally in a recent conversation about autotheory and autofiction for the MIT Press podcast (Fournier and Wark 2020).

Wark's book does a deep dive into her life as she lived it thus far, speedy and sexy, while taking a pause, every now and then, to bring in another theorist's, writer's, or artist's voice alongside. Short chunks of writings by others are incorporated into Wark's autotheoretical storytelling, block quotes that Wark, post-publication, expressed some ambivalence about including in their lengthier form, with Wark wondering whether this has become a trope of autotheory that a writer ought to resist (Fournier and Wark 2020).[1] But I think this incorporation of passages from other texts works well as a structure, creating a welcoming pace that gives a reader time and space to really absorb Wark's scenes in all their potency: the citations serve as palette cleansers of a sort, as we get ourselves into position, preparing for the next discursive/readerly fucking.

Lauren Fournier (she/they) is a writer and curator. She is the author of *Autotheory as Feminist Practice in Art, Writing, and Criticism* (2021). She holds a PhD in English literature and has published writings in journals like *Angelaki* and *Contemporary Women's Writing*. She is the director of "Fermenting Feminism," an antiracist and trans-inclusive curatorial project that takes shape transnationally. Her work has been featured and reviewed in such venues as *Columbia Journal of Literary Review*, the *New York Times*, *Art in America*, and the *Los Angeles Review of Books*. She is currently writing an autotheory of first-generation university students, of which she is one.

Note

1.   In our conversation about autotheory for the MIT Press Podcast, Wark raised the question of what constitutes good or bad autotheory. We reflected on the tropes that have arisen within autotheory as a practice or genre, and Wark made note of her own ambivalence regarding the way she used citations in her book.

Reference

Fournier, Lauren, and McKenzie Wark. 2020. MIT Press Podcast, December 7. mitpress.podbean .com/e/full-version-lauren-fournier-and-mckenzie-wark-on-autotheory/.

Transmedia Uprising

CHRISTOPHER JOSEPH LEE

Trans Exploits: Trans of Color Cultures and Technologies in Movement
Jian Neo Chen
Durham, NC: Duke University Press, 2019. 200 pp.

In a time of trans visibility predicated on the *Time* magazine's much-heralded and much-contested "transgender tipping point" (Steinmetz 2014), what role do trans culture and digital media play in deciphering or short-circuiting trans progress narratives? In *Trans Exploits*, Jian Neo Chen begins their compelling study of trans of color art and activism by reflecting on *Time*'s 2014 cover article, "The Transgender Tipping Point," observing how its "technical administering of civil rights . . . advance[s] the internal and external frontiers of American empire" (3). By exploring a range of both established and emergent artists in film/video, performance literature, and digital media, Chen pushes against the seeming absorption of the transgender subject into a new chapter of the US settler colonial narrative. As Chen argues, trans of culture artists, including those working from Black, Asian American, Latinx, and Indigenous positionalities, "address and attempt to rework . . . the technologies and histories of racial and colonial gendering that have established binary gendersex as one of the primary fault lines for securing and differentiating the national body of the white settler U.S. state and civil society" (4). In this way, Chen approaches trans of color less as a descriptor of gender or racial identity and more as a term that lights up the solidarities, kinships and, communities that spring from a shared sense of subjugation under, survival of, and resistance against state and interpersonal violence.

In working through a seemingly disparate collection of media objects, from Janet Mock's best-selling memoir, *Redefining Realness* (2014), to more experimental entries like filmmaker and performance artist Wu Tsang's "Shape of a Right Statement" (2008), Chen remains attuned to the ways in which trans of color activists and culture producers build a framework for trans embodied antiviolence practices in opposition to carceral and punitive approaches. The cohort of trans of color artists assembled in *Trans Exploits* work across digital media, print, and film/video. Some are US based, others transnational; some popular, others fringe. Chen's readings move nimbly between what could be called "high culture"—performance and installation art—and more mainstream fare, surfacing a shared interest among trans of color artists in weighing the outsized influence that colonization and capitalism play in building a rights-based framework for trans inclusion. *Trans Exploits* fits within a broader effort to build a trans political movement extending beyond legal recognition and protection. In highlighting the complexities of trans of color aesthetic and cultural responses, Chen works within the ethos of a "critical trans politics," as defined by Dean Spade: a "[political movement] that is about practice and process rather than arrival at a singular point of 'liberation'" (20).

Divided into four primary chapters, "Culture," "Networks," "Memory," and "Movement," *Trans Exploits* casts a deliberately wide net in exploring the depth of, and at times dissonances within, trans of color cultural responses. One of the richest through lines of Chen's work is their commitment to unpacking the historical resonances of the contemporary pieces and media objects that anchor their readings. In "Culture," Chen aligns three Asian American visual artists, Yozmit, Wu Tsang, and Zavé Martohardjono, as a means of observing how embodied trans practices and performances comment on the longstanding "U.S. state and social mind-body-sense regimes that have sought to extinguish, surveil, sequester, and control the multiplicity of Asian American genders" (32). In their close reading of Yozmit's live performance of a song entitled "Sound of New Pussy," Chen highlights Yozmit's interplays between the binary dichotomies that determine gender expectations. In this performance, Yozmit strips away pieces of an elaborate neo-Victorian costume that appear to conceal a hidden truth, but, as Chen argues, "each stripping away of the femme surface only reveals another femme surface that suggests depth and substance" (38). Chen observes an intermingling of interiority and exteriority that unsettles the cisnormative fixation on gender secrecy and disclosure. Chen's definition of trans experience is built on aesthetic and embodied expressions like Yozmit's, which point both to an "alienation from how one's gender has been perceived," as well as to the "various degrees and contexts of disalignment and alignment" that sit in contrast to cisgender being (38). For Chen, attending the multiplicity of unhomings encompassed in trans becoming necessitates an analysis of the enduring dislocations enacted by US empire. *Trans Exploits* highlights canonical queer markers like the 1969 Stonewall demonstrations, but it also centers the foundational importance of major historical shifts in deportation, detention, and occupation: the sanctioning of and racialization of migration through the 1965 Immigration Act, the emergence of the prison-industrial complex in the early 1970s, and the US government's recognition of and assimilation of Native self-determination under the Nixon administration. By weighing these histories in tandem, Chen connects the state management of gender and citizenship across Indigenous and racialized communities.

Trans Exploits also trains its attention to the digital infrastructures that enable increasingly networked forms of capitalism. In their second chapter, Chen argues against "neoliberal accounts of the digital economy driven by technological, economic and social determinisms," highlighting, instead, the "racially binary systems of gender, sex, and sexuality" that structure the globalization of labor and markets (60). Through close readings of Taiwanese digital media artist Cheang Shu Lea's works, including *I.K.U.* (2000), a porn ripoff of Ridley Scott's *Blade Runner*, and its multimedia sequel, *UKI* (2009–14), Chen takes stock of how new forms of embodied pleasure are both enabled and exploited by digital technologies. In *I.K.U.*, "orgasmic data" is quite literally captured and stored by corporate entities to mass-produce sexual pleasure. Chen utilizes this film's staging of gender and sexuality to think through and dispel fantasies of frictionless digital infrastructures, arguing that "there is nothing 'new,' 'post-industrial,' or 'global,' about the [information technology] economy" (71). For Chen, Cheang's work illuminates the uneven distribution of labor and extraction that fuels a seemingly "clean and equalizing high-tech global economy." Rather than follow purely dystopic or utopic accounts of networked cultures, however, Chen carves out a space for imagining new forms of play and pleasure that might, despite all odds, emerge from highly corporatized and highly controlled media technologies. In *I.K.U.*'s sequel, *UKI*, invisible sites of electronic waste and refuse become potential breeding grounds for reassembly and repurposing; *Trans Exploits* draws attention to these kinds of transformational spaces to generate an account of trans media that emphasizes open possibilities over fixed end points.

While Chen devotes much of *Trans Exploits* to addressing aesthetic interventions into racial and colonial discourses, they give equal weight to activist uses of digital technologies. In their fourth chapter, "Movement," *Trans Exploits* gathers several transnational models of trans and gender-nonconforming activism that directly engage with digital platforms and media. The first section of this chapter charts the efforts of the South African LGBTI group Iranti-org to reverse "top-down universal narratives about LGBT lives and rights" through digital video documentaries about antiqueer and racist violence (110). In addressing these videos as a kind of "vernacular documentation," Chen argues that Iranti-org offers an intimacy and depth rarely afforded the stories of murdered Black queer and trans South Africans. Although Iranti-org's videos shed a light on the violence wrought against Black LGBTI people, these videos also work to resist the conversion of antiqueer violence into raw "data and spectacle," given state-sponsored efforts to characterize LGBT rights and protections as an index for economic development (110). Chen closes this chapter on digital activism with more conceptual but no less impactful models of antiviolence support, turning to Latinx media theorist micha cárdenas's collaborative project, "Local Autonomy Networks (Autonets)." Planned across a series of workshop performances and presentations, Autonets envisions, in Chen's words, a "fashion line of mesh, networked, electronic clothing that will allow community members wearing them to communicate one's location and to respond if someone needs help" (127). Chen argues that this use of digital media amounts to both a repurposing of digital tools as well as a transformation of the very principles that "underlie U.S. technology-driven imperialism and state capitalism in the twenty-first century" (130). Rather than building out digital infrastructure to ease the movement of capital or surveillance, projects like Autonets and Iranti-org, Chen argues, utilize a variety of digital media to create community support models that work outside state and corporate frameworks.

Trans Exploits is a valuable meditation on unsettling and redefining the relationship between trans of color culture and technologies of representation. While at times overwhelming in its transnational, multimedia, and multiracial breadth, this text charts numerous points of entry for any reader interested in the converging histories of US expansion, dispossession, and detention. In addition to indexing the magnitude of violence inflicted on trans people of color both in the United States and by US imperialistic policies, *Trans Exploits* highlights the resourcefulness of trans artists and activists in building media landscapes and networks of mutual aid that contest conventional progress narratives. Indeed, it is Chen's close attention to radical activist and aesthetic imaginaries that makes *Trans Exploits* a crucial read for scholars of media studies, performance studies, and literature, as well as for any reader looking to organize political power beyond legal recognition. This text would be an equally exceptional addition to courses in critical ethnic studies, feminist theory, and digital media. Like the numerous trans cultural producers represented in Chen's work, *Trans Exploits* promises to shift the conversation around trans-embodied practices and expressions from visibility toward liberation.

Christopher Joseph Lee is a visiting assistant professor of English at Brown University, where their research explores narratives of antiqueer violence. Their writing has appeared in the *New Inquiry, Women and Performance,* and the *Baffler.*

References

Spade, Dean. 2015. *Normal Life: Administrative Violence, Critical Trans Politics, and the Limits of Law*. Durham, NC: Duke University Press.

Steinmetz, Katy. 2014. "The Transgender Tipping Point." *Time*, May 29. time.com/135480/transgender -tipping-point/.

We Build Our Own Rooms, We Build Our Own Tables

AMIR RABIYAH

We Want It All: An Anthology of Radical Trans Poetics
Edited by Andrea Abi-Karam and Kay Gabriel
New York: Nightboat Books, 2020. 454 pp.

In the opening of the anthology, *We Want It All: An Anthology of Radical Trans Poetics*, editors Andrea Abi-Karam and Kay Gabriel state that "as a collection of writing by trans people against capital and empire, this book attempts to piece together these multiple points of overlap between the subjective, interpersonal, and everyday modes of trans life, and the internalist horizons of the fights we are already engaged in" (2). This collection is firmly rooted in an anticapitalist and anti-oppressive praxis, and even includes some prominent trans trailblazers who are no longer with us, such as Sylvia Rivera, Lou Sullivan, and Leslie Feinberg.

As a trans poet who has been writing and publishing for nearly two decades, it's exciting to witness transgender and genderqueer poets get their work published and gain recognition. In the seven years since *Troubling the Line: Trans and Genderqueer Poetry and Poetics*, edited by TC Tolbert and Trace Peterson, was released, there has been an explosion of trans and genderqueer publications. This significant boom of trans literature opens up more possibilities for us as trans people, and within the genre of trans literature itself, we need varied representations of trans lives.

The challenge with any anthology is creating a sense of unity when there are so many disparate voices included. There are many styles of poetry in this anthology: narrative, formal, experimental, and ekphrastic—there are also letters, diary entries, blog posts, a speech, and prose poems. At times the collection feels disjointed, but at the same time, that's the point of the collection—to expand our

TSQ: Transgender Studies Quarterly * Volume 9, Number 1 * February 2022   **137**
DOI 10.1215/23289252-9475621   © 2022 Duke University Press

notions of what trans poetry is. There can be growth and ecstasy in disorientation, and this collection achieves both.

A number of themes and topics are covered in *We Want It All*; these are bodies of work that explore desire, lust, police brutality, abolition, capitalism, ecology, day-to-day life, identity, love, relationships, and family. Trauma is not exempt from this anthology, as in the poem "You Cannot Return a Stretched Mind." Referencing the lives lost to the AIDS epidemic, CA Conrad states, "If you could have seen my face the moment I realized no help was coming" (69), a line that could also be applied to the murders of transgender Black and brown women, which often go unacknowledged outside trans communities of color. Themes of alienation are also present, as in Trish Salah's poem "Manifest" where she writes,

> We drag our loves, we burn out raw, we passive
> aggress our families that fail us, turn us out
> We don't know where to go we shelter online
> and in shelters are refused shelter often. (399)

Salah's poem speaks to the exclusion of trans women in online spaces, but also the finding of home in these spaces. Salah is also referencing how, because of transphobic policies, trans women "are refused" entry to homeless or domestic violence shelters when attempting to find safety.

Ray Filar's prose poem/essay "You've heard of Ritalin, now what if I told you governments make bodies into crime scenes for no reason at all" is a poem that explores the medical-industrial complex, pharmaceuticals, classism, attention-deficit/hyperactivity disorder, and disability. Filar says, "Drugs name a politics of usage: the sanctioned chemical usage that produces work or reproduces the workforce, and those whose chemical usage reproduces a class of non-workers, the prison force, the unemployed, the 'junkie,' those for whom usage becomes a social marker of fear or degradation. And sometimes drugs produce resistance, the capacity to imagine rebellion" (345). Drug use, whether prescribed or not is pathologized, yet many people rely on drugs as a coping mechanism to survive or to improve their quality of life. Disability, drugs, and the medical-industrial complex are important issues to explore, and Filar does so with a vulnerability that many readers will relate to.

This anthology also embeds humor, sex, the erotic, and the surreal. For example, in Cyrée Jarelle Johnson's poem "harold mouthfucks THE DEVIL," an abusive alcoholic stepfather has a sexual encounter with the devil (who is non-binary), and the stepfather has an identity crisis, questioning their sexuality. Johnson writes,

> it's still gay to Harold. THE DEVIL values consent so they ask
>   Harold
> if he would like a fellatio and Harold nods and screams YES! YES!
>   6 covens
> of genderless magical practitioners arrive for orgies nearby
>   because THE DEVIL
> is into that. Everyone in the vicinity is on the verge of ecstasy
>   when Harold starts to cry. (120)

Charles Theonia's poem "The People's Beach" opens with the following:

> on your leash I'm accounted for
> femmes cuddle up on the sand
> you grab my ass say you like
> to see us enjoying each other (95)

There is an overall arch of unapologetic-ness that I appreciate about this collection. It does not beg for trans people to be given a seat at the table; rather, it builds multiple tables and rooms for trans people to exist in, which is refreshing and long overdue. The collection does not demand for trans people's humanity to be respected; instead it embraces a range of trans poetic narratives, and trans people's humanity is just a given. With so many types of poems in this collection, there will be several entry points for the reader to find their way in. Although there were some pieces I could not connect with because they were so experimental that I was unable to remain grounded, this anthology is diverse enough that anyone with an interest in trans writing will find themselves moved and inspired. *We Want It All* is an important contribution to the growing body of trans literature.

Amir Rabiyah is the author of the poetry collection *Prayers for My 17th Chromosome* (2017), which was a finalist for the Publishing Triangle Award and an ALA Over the Rainbow pick, and coeditor of *Writing the Walls Down: A Convergence of LGBTQ Voices* (2015). Their work has been published in numerous anthologies and journals. To learn more, visit www.amirrabiyah.com.

Chimera Project

TOBARON WAXMAN

> I'm a landlocked lad, struggling to grow a fin and swim into the great big uncertain
> sea.
> —Jax Jackson, *Chimera Project Riis Beach* participant, 2012

*C*himera Project: Riis Beach (2012) was created in response to the suicides of four trans people in spring and summer 2012.[1] The resonances of these deaths rippled through local Toronto, New York, and Chicago communities and the internet; the effect was devastating.

Chimera Project is a collaborative photography project in which trans people can participate as subject and photographer simultaneously. The photographs are attributed to all the participants, each of whom is mourning a deceased trans loved one. Each *Chimera Project* shoot is in response to local transphobic violence or the loss of a trans community member, with trans mourners and survivors aspiring to channel mourning as a generative power.

Using photography as a generative process for survivors of transphobic violence, this project uses skill sharing, oral transmission, and intergenerational collaboration as methods of building trans art histories relationally among peers. Each frame is a shared combination of performance, composition, and guided technical experimentation. Each participant confirms the boundaries of their participation, in voice, technics, and desire, with freedom to improvise and change roles as they wish.

Participants included Tobi Halberstroh, Jax Jackson, Zackary Wager Scholl, Kerry Downey, and Tinker Coalescing. The fishtail costumes were designed and fabricated by Aimée Finlay, founder of Beestung Lingerie, for *Chimera Project: Toronto* (2004).[2] Nogga Schwartz and I taught the participants night photography, painting the subject with torches, lit by the August supermoon. It was also on the

TSQ: Transgender Studies Quarterly ★ Volume 9, Number 1 ★ February 2022
DOI 10.1215/23289252-9517364   © 2022 Duke University Press

birthday of my beloved friend Flo McGarrell, a trans artist creating a unique safe haven for LGBTQ+ in Haiti, killed in the earthquakes of January 2010, to whom I dedicated my role in the shoot.

Imagining trans futures, *Chimera Project* reclaims the chimera motif from its transphobic application. As derived from various classical sources and mythologies, a chimera's sole purpose is to embody a lesson or provide "object-voice" to wisdom the hero/protagonist needs to continue his journey (Dolar 2006). As a discontiguous entity, a chimera has no purpose without a hero to encounter and is not the protagonist in its own story. It exists only to dazzle in the realm of the fantastical/symbolic, not as a person—with lovers, family, friends.

The silvery light in long exposure creates images that shimmer in simultaneous darkness and brightness as an analogy to the complexities of a lived trans life. The camera's historic relationship to queer bodies, as a pathologizing and colonizing tool, is counteracted; rather than "taking" a picture, we are "making" an image,[3] while exchanging memories and wisdom inherited from our friends who passed away. The spirit of *Chimera Project* is t4t; creating possibility together via a horizontal model of intergenerational skill sharing, oral histories, and play as queer sustainability tactics.

Whenever I travel, I feel compelled to bring the mermaid costumes. I travel only when invited to be an artist-scholar somewhere, for a month, or six, or eleven. In the likelihood that I will meet other trans people who are mourning a trans loved one lost to suicide, bashing, cancer, medical neglect, I can propose to them *Chimera Project*. I ask participants to bring as many cameras as they can and, in memory and celebration of our dead friends, please, "tell me what you learned from Aligül (Istanbul) and I can tell you what I learned from Flo (Haiti), regardless of how little else we have in common, we all have unresolved anguish, love, and laughter for our dead friends. I want to learn about your friend, and I want to share with you about my friend. To take the unspent churning energy of mourning and do something with it, despite the religious traditions that rejected you."

*   *   *

Thus far there have been three *Chimera Project* collaborations in Toronto, Brooklyn, and Istanbul.

Exhibition History

"Mentors" exhibition, CFHill, Stockholm, December 8, 2016–January 6, 2017, curated by Rick Herron.

Publication History

"Mentors" exhibition catalogue, CFHill, Stockholm, 2016. www.tobaron.com/cfh
   _mentors_cat_final/.

"Chimera Project," Jordan Arsenault, *2BMagazine* 10, no. 7.

Collections

Private collections in Canada, Sweden, the Netherlands, and New York.

Tobaron Waxman (Tkaronto/Brooklyn) is an interdisciplinary artist and curator who sings. Tobaron's projects investigate how the state imposes borders and parameters on bodies and lands. Their works have been exhibited at such venues as Palais de Tokio, Videotage Hong Kong, Kunsthalle Vienna, FestivAlt Krakow, the New Museum, the Leslie Lohman Museum of Gay and Lesbian Art, and Brooklyn College Conservatory of Music and via fellowships at Van Lier, New York; Akademie der Künste der Welt, Cologne; and Kulturlabor ICI Berlin Institute of Cultural Inquiry. Developing theory on trans vocality as a vocalist, Tobaron has sung liturgy in hospitals and at memorials and weddings as well as performed at Kampnagel Festival of Choreography and Protest Hamburg, Donau Festival, and Dixon Place, New York. In 2013, Tobaron founded the Intergenerational LGBT Artist Residency as a combined curatorial, relational/live art, and sociopolitical praxis. ILGBTAR also functions as a curatorial consultancy, collaborating with museums and galleries internationally. Since 2017 Tobaron has lead the Trans Collections at The ArQuives, as part of a collaborative team at the largest independent LGBTQ archive in the world. Tobaron's writing and photography have been published internationally, including in *Carte Blanche* (2006), *Post Porn Politics* (2010), *Fast Feminism* (2010), and *Trans Bodies Trans Selves* (2014), and have featured in such publications as *Oxford Bibliographies, Missy, C Magazine, Fuse, Canadian Dimension, Canadian Theatre Review, Lillith, Women and Performance, GLQ, TSQ,* and *LTTR*. Tobaron is the 2022–23 artist in residence at Polin Museum/Teatr Powszechny Warsaw as part of the SSHRC project Thinking through the Museum: A Partnership Approach to Curating Difficult Knowledge in Public.

Notes

1.   Marc Aguhar, Kyle Scanlon, Leo O'Hanlon, and Xavier Ruiz Caldo Flores (DJ Sirlinda).
2.   *Chimera Project: Toronto* took place in a swimming pool in Toronto, with materials from the now defunct Goodwill sewn in philosopher Shannon Bell's (*Fast Feminism*) kitchen.
3.   A distinction I learned from Del LaGrace Volcano.

Reference

Dolar, Mladen. 2006. *A Voice and Nothing More.* Cambridge, MA: MIT Press.